THE NEW CREATION: MARXIST AND CHRISTIAN?

ORBIS BOOKS
Maryknoll, New York 10545

THE NEW CREATION: MARXIST AND CHRISTIAN?

JOSE-MARIA GONZALEZ-RUIZ

TRANSLATED BY MATTHEW J. O'CONNELL

Originally published as *Marxismo y cristianismo frente al hombre nuevo* by Editorial Fontanella, Barcelona, and Ediciones Marova, Madrid

Manufactured in the United States of America

Library of Congress Cataloging in Publication Data

González-Ruiz, José María, 1916-
    The new creation.

    Translation of Marxismo y cristianismo frente al hombre nuevo.
    Includes bibliographical references.
    1. Christian life—1960-   2. Communism and Christianity.   3. Christian ethics.   I. Title.
BV4506.G6613   248'.4   76-10226
ISBN 0-88344-3279

CONTENTS

PREFACE TO
THE U.S. EDITION

When everybody uses a word, it becomes quite difficult to reach agreement on its meaning or to discuss that meaning in an even-tempered, reasonable way. This has been the fate of the words "Marxism" and "Christianity."

Over a long period of time Christians have gotten used to speaking of "atheistic Marxism." As a result, they have come to believe that there is no point in trying to establish any genuine contact between Marxism and Christianity. The one, after all, rejects what the other regards as its very essence. There can indeed be various kinds of cooperation between those who happen to be Christians and Marxists respectively, but a Christian can never be a Marxist.

In this book I am attempting to get beyond this simplistic contrast with its rather academic overtones and to raise a very realistic question: Will "the new person" be Christian or Marxist?

In putting the question I am, of course, using the very terms that our contemporaries consider to be strictly contradictory of one another. At the same time, however, I am convinced that a rereading of Karl Marx, on the one hand, and a more careful reading of the biblical sources of Christianity, on the other, will force us to transcend the contradiction and reject the necessity of choosing one or other of two absolutely exclusive alternatives: Marxist *or* Christian.

It is the Latin Americans who have perhaps best succeeded in ridding the terms "Christianity" and "Marxism" of their respective sacral and satanic overtones. They have come to see that Marxist atheism, if it is to be genuinely revolutionary and properly "Marxist," cannot be taken as requiring an unconditional metaphysical rejection of God as the Other, the Wholly Other.

Enrique Dussel has pointed out that Feuerbach and Marx—but not Kierkegaard in his lucid critique of Christendom from the viewpoint of Christianity—identified Hegel's "god" (who was nothing but the apotheosis of the European ego in its imperial and more recently its capitalist embodiments) with "god" as such.[1] Marx was faced with a system that had already been divinized or turned into an idol, and with a religion that had become totally identified with its European form and therefore had no place for a God who is Other, who causes change, who orders history to a goal. Marx therefore thought of all religion as being *the religion of European Christendom* (it did not matter whether it was Catholic, Lutheran, or Calvinist). Thinking that the problem of God was now settled, he calmly turned to human beings; he believed that there would now be no temptation to idolatry. He failed to realize, however, that the "theism" he was so stubbornly resisting was in fact a negation of another theism: that of the God who is Other.

Dussel concludes: "Marx, like all the prophets, rejects an idolatrous 'god' (in this case, money); in this form, atheism makes perfect sense. On the positive side, however, Marx (like Feuerbach) affirmed only man, and that in a socialist fashion. He did not realize that he was paving the way for the sacralization of the first socialism to come along."

Marx's outlook was a fairly narrow one. He did not realize that religious consciousness would continue to function after the coming of messianic socialism, nor did he foresee that a way would have to be found of preventing the new religious consciousness from becoming just as fetishist as the old. The capitalist bourgeoisie, however, welcomed this naive and radical error of the socialists with open arms, for they realized that it had left them free to manipulate the Christian consciousness. And that it proceeded to do wonderfully well.

Now that prophets from both worlds, formerly kept strictly apart, have come to know each other and talk to each other, they have realized that the problem they had conjured up was a false one. There is no reason why there must be Christians *and* Marxists, since the revolutionary content of Marxism can be taken over by the Christian, while the Christian faith can be adopted by one who hitherto has been a classical-style Marxist. The "theism-atheism" alternatives which distinguished and separated Christian and Marxist have turned out to be a mighty "Berlin wall" built by the two blocs which a far-reaching rivalry had formed.

Christians have been ridding themselves of their obsession with "Marxist atheism" and coming to see that the image of the new person, as the Christian conceives it, is not *of itself* contrary to the Marxist image of the person. What does continue to mark that image of the new person is a prophetic dynamism in the face of all the Vaticans and Kremlins of our confused world.

In this book I am attempting, then, to go beyond the historical dialogues between "Christians" and "Marxists" and to present in a straightforward way the vision of the new person that is to be found in the authentic sources of Christianity.

As Christians, we have nothing but our faith and hope to help us face the future with confidence; therefore, I shall avoid all pseudo-prophecy, which is nothing but naive guesswork.

This much, admittedly, can be predicted: We shall not be able to speak in the immediate future of a Christian Marxism or a Marxist Christianity. But we shall indeed see everywhere Marxists who regard themselves as Christians, and Christians who have chosen Marxism and are struggling to put it into practice.

There is no point in wasting time with the question: "Who will win out: the Christians or the Marxists?" That kind of question is simply an anachronistic diversion for people who, though still "alive," have ceased to look to the future and to hope in it.

We shall be reading Paul and the Gospels. We shall be reflecting in the company of Someone who urges us forward, and hoping in that Other who has not been programmed by our computers.

NOTES

1. Enrique Dussel, "El ateismo de los profetas y Marx," *Misiones Extranjeras* (Madrid), nos. 22–23 (1974).

INTRODUCTION

I

If the reader is to put this book into its proper perspective, we must begin by defining accurately the terms in which its questions and propositions are framed.

"Marxism" and "Christianity" are, both of them, ambivalent words, each carrying very different historical overtones and awakening deeply divergent feelings.

By way of entering fully into our major theme, we must observe that the comparison we are making between "Marxism" and "Christianity" is strictly between the two as "ideologies." For, historically speaking, Christianity and Marxism have been, and continue to be, authentic ideologies.

We shall pass over the various other senses in which the word "ideology" is used and adhere to the usual Marxist acceptation of it. Louis Althusser provides a definition that we shall take as our starting point: "An ideology is a system (with its own logic and rigour) of representations (images, myths, ideas or concepts, depending on the case) endowed with a historical existence and role within a given society."[1]

Althusser goes on to say:

In every society we can posit, in forms which are sometimes very paradoxical, the existence of an economic activity as the base, a political organization and "ideological" forms (religion, ethics, philosophy, etc.). *So ideology is as such an organic part of every social totality.* It is as if human societies could not survive without these *specific formations,* these systems of representations (at various levels), their ideologies. Human societies secrete ideology as the very element and atmosphere indispensable to their historical respiration and life. Only an ideological world outlook could have imagined societies *without ideology* and accepted the utopian idea of a world in which ideology (not just one of its

1

historical forms) would disappear without trace, to be replaced by *science*. For example, this utopia is the principle behind the idea that ethics, which is in its essence ideology, could be replaced by science or become scientific through and through; or that religion could be destroyed by science which would in some way take its place; that *art* could merge with knowlege or become "everyday life," etc.[2]

Following the logic of his position, Althusser admits that the inevitability of ideology applies to Marxism too: "I am not going to steer clear of the crucial question: *historical materialism cannot conceive that even a communist society could ever do without ideology, be it ethics, art or 'world outlook.'* "[3]

We may note, finally, that Althusser stresses the necessary consequence of his positions: that if we are really determined to defend an existing science against the ideology that threatens it, it is important to determine what really forms part of *ideology*; otherwise we may end up by mistaking something genuinely scientific for part of an ideology.[4]

II

The confusion between the scientific and the ideological is a constant danger, according to Marxism, in the various kinds of thinking that claim to offer a comprehensive view of reality. Felice Balbo provides a penetrating analysis of this confusion. He notes that "in such religious formulations as are most influenced by mythology the lack of critical distinctions and, more generally, of a developed critical awareness, allows religion to give a mythical explanation of the world, nature, and history; this aspect of religion has made it vulnerable to attack by all forms of historicism."[5] In other words: "Religious visions of the world and history confuse mystery with problem, and *all reality* with all that is known or proved."[6]

It is true enough that religion has, quite typically, passed from the ideological order into the scientific and that it has been replaced by a kind of theological rationalism. More specifically: God has been turned into "God" or a fetish. "God" (the quotation marks indicate that we mean a corrupted version of God) was, at bottom, a hypostatized projection of human frustrations and as such provided a false explanation of these frustrations and prevented any scientific, objective search for a solution to them. Balbo continues:

When God is used as a "working hypothesis," he is no longer God but simply a word turned into a hypostasis, a fetish that, in the judgment of the contemporary world, simply makes a mystification both of God and world. When the human being believes in God as a working hypothesis, he hypostatizes, fixes, and absolutizes this hypothesis so that it becomes incapable of verification, criticism, and development, or, in a word, of any dialectic. It is thereby rendered useless as a means of interpreting and transforming the world and history.[7]

When religion has so degenerated, the charge of "religious alienation" levelled at it by Feuerbach, Marx, and all schools of Marxist thought is basically justified. "God" becomes a barrier to human self-development and must be removed. In the first stage of the dialogue between atheistic Marxists and Christian believers it became clear that believers have ceased to accept "God" as the object of their faith. They have admitted that the authentic content of their religious awareness forces them to reject a "God-of-the-gaps" or "God-the-immanent-explanation-of-evolution," and to admit only the transcendent God who is not part of the world, although he is freely present in the world and readily apprehended by faith.

Balbo is right in saying that this elimination of "God," which Marxism brought about in its struggle against religious alienation, is the result of a strictly *scientific* process. Up to this point the behavior of *scientific reason,* which underlies all the analyses carried out by historical materialism, is quite justified. But there comes a moment in which an illogical passage is made from *scientific reason* to *absolute scientific reason.* Concretely, not only is "God" eliminated (by a strictly scientific process capable of justifying itself), but it is also maintained, in an a priori fashion, that the elimination of God is required if the self-realization of humankind is to be asserted in theory and in practice. This illogical jump Balbo calls "atheistic alienation" or "worldly alienation."

From a *scientific* standpoint, it is true that the person must be defined by his economic relationships. But it is also true, and from a no less scientific point of view, that these economic relations do not exhaust the reality of the person.

It is a *historical fact* that people look to God for a fulfillment beyond the real limits they now experience. Scientific reason may pass only an after-the-fact judgment on this fact of religion; it has no right to an a priori pseudometaphysical judgment that God has definitively died at some given moment in the evolution of humankind.

In other words, when belief in God claims to take the place of scientific reason, it is trespassing. But the same thing happens when scientific reason moves outside the limits set by its own kind of verifiability and makes statements that are both unjustified for it and pseudometaphysical as well, while acting as though it were making scientifically verifiable claims.

A religious ideology that gets itself accepted as scientific profanes God's transcendence by reducing it to the level of reason. But, by the same token, a purely sociological ideology that includes among its supposedly verifiable statements a denial of the transcendent unduly sacralizes its strictly scientific presuppositions, which belong to the secular order.

III

At this point, we must recognize the fact that scientific theories have been preceded by and have even originated in prescientific ideologies.

The Italian Marxist Lucio Lombardo-Radice makes a profound and penetrating distinction in this area between philosophies, understood as "working hypotheses," and scientific theories, which historically have sprung from the philosophies. At the moment when the scientific theories are formulated, there is a close connection between science and ideology. But once a science has achieved a sufficient measure of verification, it must break the umbilical cord that connects it with the originating prescientific intuitions and become a wholly *secular* tool, that is, one that is now independent of the hypothesis that led to its existence. Lombardo-Radice believes that all science is secular in nature and therefore compatible with philosophies different from those that played a determining role in the origin of the science itself.

The Italian thinker courageously draws the inescapable conclusion from his basic distinction: Dialectical materialism served as the general philosophical hypothesis that enabled Marx to make his own great discovery of the "law of the movement of history." Once the discovery was made, it became a *secular* truth that imposed itself on people who accepted the most varied philosophies, as a valid description and key to understanding of a real process, or as *knowledge* that has its intrinsic value and is independent of the philosophical hypothesis that triggered its discovery. The scientific principle, despite its strictly *secular* character, of course, cannot but continue to be related to the philosophical hypothesis from which it emerged, but its validity in no way requires *acceptance* of the philosophical intuition.[8]

In a discussion with the German Communist Max Friedrich (who demanded a strict kind of Marxist "confessionalism"), Lombardo-Radice urged Friedrich and others of like mind to face up to new facts like good revolutionaries and good Marxists.

Camilo Torres has a *Weltanschauung* or view of the world that derives not from dialectical materialism but from Christianity, the latter being understood along the lines of a particular theology ("love of God coinciding with love of neighbor," to use Karl Rahner's words). It was *this* conception of the world that led him to become a revolutionary; *since* adopting this new position he has lived (and died!) as a wonderfully *integrated* man, being both Christian and revolutionary.[9]

IV

The frame of mind expressed by Lombardo-Radice, which is a strictly correct one in the Marxist universe of thought, corresponds to a similar outlook which we Catholic theologians are now adopting in absolute fidelity to the essential reference points of the Christian faith.

Lombardo-Radice himself quotes the following words from an earlier book of mine and sees expressed in them an outlook quite parallel to his own position as a Marxist: "Our God, the living God of Abraham, Isaac, and Jacob, never presents himself to us in the Bible as an immanent key to cosmic and human reality; on the contrary, he is always an immense question mark over our lives and never becomes a concrete, exhaustive answer."[10]

Sociologists acknowledge that Christianity, as a working hypothesis or vision of the world, has as a matter of historical fact generated a whole series of values and methods for social change that are now fully naturalized in the world of the humane sciences. There is, for example, the sense of universal brotherhood, of democracy, and of the one human adventure shared by all. Such values, though springing from Christian intuitions, had to acquire full autonomy and become *secular* realities. It was not always so. The Middle Ages gave birth to a system of human relations within whose frontiers a person had to profess the Christian faith if he was to be a first-class citizen. Non-Christians could only be tolerated as second- or third-class citizens; this was the lot of the Jews who were locked in their ghettos and prohibited from exercising public office and owning real estate.

This aspect of medieval fanaticism can exist in a new form today, according to Lombardo-Radice, but on the non-Christian side. If it does, it will seriously hinder the universal spread of "historical materialism" or "Marxist sociology." The danger is in requiring an antecedent "Marxist faith" (the acceptance of dialectical materialism or its vision of the world, which includes atheism) as a condition for being a first-class citizen in a revolutionary country or a front-rank revolutionary in the effort toward human liberation.

It is clear then that neither valid and stringent self-reflection on the part of Marxism as a science nor a valid Christian theology will allow us to turn scientific value systems or scientific methods of social change into "confession." This is so even though, historically speaking, the values and methods arose out of philosophical intuitions.

V

The point we are making is that *militant scientific atheism is no less alienating than militant scientific theism.* Neither the profession of faith in a transcendent God nor the rejection of this faith can claim to be a necessary premise for total integration into a revolutionary movement. An atheistic revolutionary has no scientific basis for claiming in an a priori way that the believer who may be accepted into a revolutionary movement must cease to be a believer if his adherence to the revolution is to deepen and become permanent. Such a claim is not scientific at all, but an arbitrary piece of metaphysics that has no place in the area reserved for reason and verification.

But, in the same way, a revolutionary who is also a believer has no scientific basis for the a priori claim that the atheistic revolutionary must inevitably cease to be an atheist by reason of the intrinsic demands of the revolutionary process itself. In other words, confessionalism (be it theistic or atheistic) is the great obstacle to human coexistence in the near future. Coexistence necessarily requires pluralism.

In building the new "secular city" for which we all yearn, people cannot be subject to discrimination because of their belief or disbelief in God. Moreover, believers should have no difficulty in collaborating in social, political, and economic movements, even when these originated in a philosophical vision that was atheistic and that they find thoroughly unacceptable. Here we have one of the major intuitions of Pope John XXIII: "It is perfectly legitimate to make a clear distinction between a false philosophy of the nature, origin and purpose of men and the world, and economic, social, cultural and political undertakings, even when such undertakings draw their origin and inspiration from that philosophy" (*Pacem in Terris*, no. 159). This is precisely the thesis I am defending; for dialectical materialism gave rise to historical materialism or Marxist sociology. The pope leaves Catholics free to embrace such movements on condition that they do not accept the philosophical doctrines that gave rise to the movements. The only further condition the pope sets down is that such political, economic, or cultural movements should not impede or smother the spiritual values that the Church regards as essential for the preservation of Christian belief; this amounts to saying that the movements should not become "confessional" in the direction of militant atheism.

VI

We now have the starting point for the reflections offered in this book. It can be expressed by saying that, even though all take for granted a genuinely pluralistic practical behavior that is exempt from any taint of confessionalism, the *ideology* that gave rise to such a praxis exists and will continue to exist.

In other words, believers and nonbelievers may have reached full accord in a unified praxis aimed at social change, but there is still a difference between them, and the difference is not reducible to something private and intimate within each but affects the way they coexist in a group.

The human being is not reducible to the reality (unmistakably primordial though it is) of his social relations and rational verifiability. Ileana Marculescu, professor of Marxist philosophy at Bucharest, recently admitted to the Christians at a Christian-Marxist meeting in Geneva: "We Marxists have sold short the element of mystery." She said this, not in order to induce us to "rationalize" the element of mystery, but simply that we might share with her the existential reality of our experience of this mystery.

Within the consciousness of all people living today there is a conviction concerning, and a preoccupation with, the "new person" who is being brought to birth amid the birth pangs caused by a tremendously accelerated change from one historical epoch to another. What will the "new person" be like?

I do not think that Christianity, as such, must enter among the competitors in the marketplace and offer a *rational, scientific* model of the "new person." That is not the mission of Christianity. Believers, after all, are people like others, and their faith does not lead to a special type of humanness. We Christians, says Vatican II, "are witnesses of the birth of a new humanism, one in which man is defined first of all by his responsibility toward his brothers and toward history" (*Gaudium et Spes,* no. 55).

On the other hand, we Christians would fall victim to a silly inferiority complex and serve humankind very badly if we were to be bashful and hide the tremendous riches that our religious consciousness represents.

As believers, we must ask pardon for the times we have profaned the ideological (prescientific) aspect of our faith by trying to make of it a rational, scientific factor in the autonomous search being carried on in the human mind. At the same time, however, we must strongly criticize the illogical and illicit claim of those who have turned *scientific reason* into an *absolute scientific reason.*

In this contest of humility, believers and nonbelievers now confront each other. We believers cannot but humbly communicate to our brothers and sisters the riches contained in our faith experience. At the same time, we are aware that God alone can enter the sanctuary of the human conscience; for this reason we dare only approach the vestibule in a gentle way and knock respectfully on the door of all our human brothers and sisters, whatever their color.

VII

The following reflections on the Christian meaning of human development claim only to be the reflections of one Christian. Their point of reference is the theology of the New Testament, and especially the splendid views of St. Paul on the "new person." An attentive reading of the Pauline letters will once again bring light into many darkened sectors of our ancient Christian communities, where alarming symptoms of division are now being manifested.

Unfortunately, many former Christians experienced their crisis because of a falsified, even caricatural presentation of the real message of salvation that Christ brought and proclaimed to the world. That message we find in the deathless pages of the New Testament, which expresses the reflective awareness of the first generation of Christians.

In the unassuming pages which follow we intend to stand before the Truth as humble disciples. For, in point of fact, the main reason why the Truth eludes us is that we attempt to imprison it and cut it to fit the narrow limits of our own private world. But the Truth utterly transcends any single person, and the only way to properly direct ourselves toward it is to admit this transcendence unreservedly. The Truth cannot be cut down to size by attaching a possessive adjective to it. It belongs neither to me nor to you, neither to the wise nor to the elect. It is beyond and above any one of us, and all of us alike are its servants.

For this reason it would be a sacrilege for any of us to claim a monopoly on the distribution of the Truth, for no person is big enough to pocket the immeasurable greatness of Truth. There are, of course, people who proclaim the Truth. But to carry out their sublime task takes an almost infinite humility. Such people must tremble with fear at having been chosen, without any merit on their part, to tap their brothers and sisters gently on the shoulder and point out to them, in all modesty, the point on the horizon where the light is breaking.

The person who proclaims the Truth must not come as a superior being and mount the professor's dais, there to call for the attention of the passing human throngs. No, he must be part of the immense caravan of life, share its fortunes, rejoice in its victories, feel anguish at its tragedies, be humble before its greatness. And when he offers Truth to his companions on the journey, he must do so with a gesture of humility, as one who from the heart asks their pardon for his loving boldness. Above all, he must try to be one with his fellows in their purpose of pursuing the Truth. He must link arms with them and set out as their equal on the road that leads to the light.

At one point in history, the Truth became flesh in a man and was called Jesus of Nazareth. He told us, his disciples, how we are to proclaim the Truth:

The scribes and the Pharisees have succeeded Moses as teachers; therefore, do everything and observe everything they tell you. But do not follow their example. Their words are bold but their deeds are few. They bind up heavy loads, hard to carry, to lay on other men's shoulders, while they themselves will not lift a finger to budge them. All their works are performed to be seen. They widen their phylacteries and wear huge tassels. They are fond of places of honor at banquets and the front seats in synagogues, of marks of respect in public and of being called "Rabbi." As to you, avoid the title "Rabbi." One among you is your teacher, the rest are learners. Do not call anyone on earth your father. Only one is your father, the One in heaven. Avoid being called teachers. Only one is your teacher, the Messiah. The greatest among you will be the one who serves the rest [Matt. 23:2–11].

Our great contemporary poet, Antonio Machado Ruiz, was able to condense this teaching of the Gospel into a short stanza:

> Your truth? No, the Truth,
> come now with me to seek it.
> As for your own, keep it.[11]

NOTES

1. Louis Althusser, *For Marx,* trans. Ben Brewster (New York: Random House, 1969), p. 231.

2. Ibid., p. 232.

3. Ibid.

4. Ibid., p. 172.

5. Felice Balbo, "Religione e ideologia," *Opere 1954–1964* (Turin: Boringhieri, 1966), p. 233.

6. Ibid.

7. Ibid.

8. Lucio Lombardo-Radice, *Socialismo e libertà* (Rome: Riuniti, 1968), pp. 217ff.

9. Ibid., p. 204.

10. José María González-Ruiz, *El cristianismo no es un humanismo: para una teología del mundo* (Madrid: Península, 1966), p. 213.

11. *Proverbs and Songs,* no. 85, trans. in Alice Jane McVen, *Antonio Machado* (New York: Hispanic Society of America, 1959), p. 203.

CHAPTER 1

THE MARXIST CRITIQUE
OF CHRISTIAN FAITH

It may seem strange that Marxism, as a sociological phenomenon, should condition the way in which we conceive the Christian faith. The latter seems, after all, at least at first sight, to be something fixed and changeless, the same for all times and places. Nonetheless, the fact of the conditioning is inescapable, and reflection on it will lead us directly into our theme.

Christianity is not essentially and most radically different from other religions by reason of its ideological (dogmatic and moral) content, but by reason of its reference to a real event that took place within history and has been effective within it to the point of giving that history a meaning and fulfillment. The event is the salvation brought by Christ.

The word "salvation" is here understood in a very full human sense. In the view of Christianity, as we shall see further on, the person is all of a piece. It is not possible to distinguish in him, as Hellenism did, between a matter from which we may and ought to prescind and a spirit which constitutes the whole of the human person. The person, for Christianity, is the whole person as he manifests himself in the reality of every day and every moment.

But the person is also a being that is thrown into a life that constantly eludes his grasp. He wants to shape himself and makes immense efforts along this line, but the result is always disillusioning. Marxist philosophy has turned the word "alienation" or "estrangement" into a technical term for describing the state of the person insofar as he is bound by inhibiting external forces that prevent him from becoming himself. The redemption or ransom of the person refers to his definitive liberation from these restraints that hinder him on his way to self-fulfillment.

Christianity is essentially God's proclamation of total human liberation and therefore of the definitive elimination of all forms of human alienation. "Go back and report to John what you hear and see: The blind recover their sight, cripples walk, lepers are cured, the deaf hear, dead men are raised to life, and the poor have the good news preached to them" (Matt. 11:4–5).

In the biblical view, moral and physical wretchedness are closely connected, and full human liberation implies the definitive elimination of both. Christ has made redemption or ransom from sin and death possible, and Christianity consists precisely in the proclamation of this saving event, which took its rise in the person of Christ but must continue to be made effective throughout history by a handful of other people.

Theology is reflection on this event, which permeates the whole of history and deposits within it the seed that shall really bear fruit in the form of true human fulfillment.

Since this salvation works from within in the form of a vital development, it is inevitable that the people of each generation should look anxiously to those who claim to possess a formula for salvation. That is what we Christians are: possessors of a formula (the only definitive one) for complete human salvation.

Theology is an answer to the quest of living people who are shaping their lives in a particular direction. Although the saving event is the same throughout time and space, the quest of each generation has its distinct existential coloring and therefore requires an answer that is adapted to its situation. Here is where theology must inevitably change, for we cannot answer the burning questions of our contemporaries in ways whose existential tonality is derived from various past ages.

The first and most urgent obligation of a theologian is, therefore, to listen patiently to the anxious questions of his contemporaries, wherever these questions are voiced: in fiction, in philosophy, amid the noise of machines, in the conversation of the tavern, in international conferences. Forgetfulness of this serious obligation has enabled so powerful a force as Marxism to bring against

Christianity a series of objections which, at first sight, seem astonishingly strong.

Moreover, the routine and jaundiced answers—often given in modern times to the questions of people who are ever more aware of their capacity for development—have made possible a ridiculous dialogue of the deaf between lazy theologians with their hackneyed answers and a few restless people who claim to have found the secret of the ascending course of history.

Before entering upon a direct examination of the Christian message of salvation, we will listen calmly to the Marxist objections directed against Christianity and its value for fostering the human development for which people and peoples of every type are yearning.

"GOD IS A REFLECTION OF HUMAN LIFE INSOFAR AS IT IS BEYOND OUR CONTROL"

The Christian solution to the problem of human alienation is unacceptable to the Marxist. For Christianity, there is no important distinction to be made between the human and the nonhuman: The person is alienated radically and in his totality; original sin wholly permeates the person; both the human and the nonhuman are seen as alienated from eternal truth and fallen from the divine.

Christianity (as thus interpreted) is guilty of confusing the human and the divine. It teaches that the historical human situation as such is the "other," the "alien thing," that must be left behind if the person is to come fully to himself; in other words, the person can achieve his fulfillment only in God. Human alienation consists in the fall from a divine state. To overcome this alienation the person must set his course toward a God who is beyond history and in whose bosom he will reach the fulfillment proper to him.

Feuerbach was the first to criticize this supposed Christian solution. In his view, this was nothing but a naive self-deception, with the person shutting his eyes to his own tragic situation and dreaming of an ideal person. He conceives this ideal person of his dreams either as a transcendent god or else as an ultramundane status to be attained. In this way the poor wretched beggar on earth remains content with his rags and dreams his delusory dreams of encounter with the divine, dreams that are but a mirage in the arid desert of human existence.

The divine being is nothing else than the human being, or, rather, the human nature purified, freed from the limits of the individual man, made objective—i.e., contemplated and revered as another, a distinct being. All the attributes of the divine nature are, therefore, attributes of the human nature.[1]

Marx comes to the same conclusion: The life religion offers is only a projection of human wretchedness; it is in fact too pitiable for us willingly to put up with the alienations we experience in the politico-religious world. We have to turn Paul's words around and say that the wretched "glory" of the religious heaven cannot make up for our sufferings on earth (cf. Rom. 8:18). "*Religious* suffering is at the same time an *expression* of real suffering and a *protest* against real suffering. Religion is the sigh of the oppressed creature, the sentiment of a heartless world, and the soul of soulless conditions. It is the *opium* of the people."[2]

According to Marxism, then, the Christian solution must be seen as a problem, and this at a radical level. For Christianity, the divine (which achieves its ends behind the veil of this temporal and contingent world) is the truly human; the "other" (that which causes alienation) is the historical situation itself.

Starting with this interpretation of what Christianity is supposedly about, the Marxist inverts the terms. Now the divine is the "other," that which alienates the person and holds him back from the ascensional movement of development and improvement which is a genuine possibility for him. In so doing, religion becomes a "fetish," that is, a troubling illusion that keeps the person in a state of deception and prevents him from seeking within himself the means of throwing off the poison that permeates his being. Religion is, therefore, a narcotic, an opium, which keeps the person in a state of unconsciousness in which he dreams of a paradise beyond time and space; but the paradise is simply the creature of his own imagination.

In Lenin's view, religious escapism is such a hindrance to human development that the eradication of religious sentiment must be effected before any effective struggle for progress can be undertaken. He writes:

Fear created the gods (*primus in orbe deos fecit timor,* says Petronius). Fear of the blind power of capital (blind because the masses of the people cannot anticipate its workings) which at every moment in the life of the proletarian or small proprietor threatens to bring, and does bring him up against some sudden, unexpected, purely chance catastrophe that ruins him, turns him into beggar, pauper, or prostitute, and lets him die of hunger. Here we have the root of modern religion, and the materialist must keep that in mind before and above all else if he does not want to remain a novice in materialism. No book, however popularly written, can root out the religion of the masses who have been brutalized by capitalist exploitation and are ever subject to the blind destructive forces of capitalism, until these masses first learn, on their own, to struggle in a united, organized, systematic, and conscious way, against the power of capitalism in all its aspects.[3]

In Lenin's words this reproach of religion turns into a demagogic attack upon theism, and an effective one:

The weakness of the exploited classes in the struggle against those who exploit them inevitably engenders belief in a better life beyond the grave, just as the weakness of the savage in the struggle against nature engenders belief in gods, demons, miracles, etc. Religion preaches humility and resignation in this world to those who spend their lives on earth in toil and wretchedness; it consoles them with the hope of a reward in heaven. On the other hand, to those who live by the toil of others religion teaches the virtue of beneficence during their earthly lives; thus it offers them an easy justification for their exploitative activity and sells them cut-rate tickets which will admit them to heavenly blessedness. Religion is the opium of the people. Religion is a kind of spiritual intoxicant that hides from the slaves of capital their own human personality and their rights to a life worthy of human beings. But the slave who has become aware that his own liberation is possible is already only half a slave. The modern worker who has achieved self-awareness and has been educated by large-scale industry and has come to know his way around in urban life sheds his religious prejudices and has only contempt for them. He lets the priests and the bourgeois churchgoers have their heaven; for himself he seeks a better life on earth. The modern proletarian aligns himself with socialism, which calls upon science to fight against religious obscurantism and frees the worker from belief in a life beyond the grave; it organizes his energies for an effective struggle to bring about a better life on earth.[4]

This last sentence sums up the whole motivating idea behind the Marxist critique of religion: The person's self-projection into another world makes impossible his immediate development in the present world. Later on, we shall use this point as a focus for our own theological analysis of the integral human salvation that Christ has brought.

"CHRISTIANITY IS A VISION OF THE PERSON AND THE WORLD WHICH IS VALUELESS FOR THE PROGRESS OF HISTORY"

Marxist philosophers have often accused Christians of using magic in an effort to do away with, or at least gloss over, the real present evils that afflict humankind. Instead of tilling the soil, building irrigation systems, and using better fertilizers, Christians have taken to walking with hieratic step among the withered flowers and leafless trees, celebrating liturgies of evasion, raising their hands to a hypothetical heaven, and vainly pronouncing exorcisms upon the locusts who devour the land.

A world view is a comprehensive vision and complete doctrine of human nature. In a sense, a world view is what traditionally would be called a philosophy, but the term "world view" has a broader meaning than does the term "philosophy." To begin with, a world view implies an *action,* that is, something more than a mere "philosophic stance." Even when the action is not expressly formulated nor expressly linked to the doctrine, even when the bond between doctrine and action remains implicit and the action does not give rise to a *program,* the action nonetheless does exist. In the Christian world view the action is Church politics and arises out of decisions taken by Church authorities; even though it does not have a *rational* link with a rational doctrine, this action is fully real. In the Marxist world view, action is rationally defined in connection with a whole body of doctrine and gives rise *openly* to a political program. . . .

No one today would think of denying, nor is there any need to prove, that Catholicism is a political doctrine, or, in other words, that the Church has a politics of its own. But insufficient attention is paid to the nature of the link between politics and doctrine. We must dwell on this point for a moment. Is the link perhaps a rational one? No. From religious propositions it is impossible to deduce, in a rational way, propositions concerning the state and social structure. The same impossibility holds when the starting point is abstract, metaphysical propositions concerning a hierarchy of "substances." The connection is a purely factual one, and the political applications remain extrinsic to the metaphysical principles. Between the two levels of thought there exists no relation that can be rationally determined. This, of course, has the advantage that it allows great freedom in maneuvering.[5]

The accusation is a serious one and we cannot simply ignore it. It is saying that Christianity is a vision of the person and the world which *of itself* has no influence on the historical progress of the world through time. If the Church does have a program, it elaborates it on the spur of the moment and without any relation to its creed. Dogma has an honored place, off in a splendid but distant niche, where incense is offered by a few priestly figures who have for the moment set aside all vital, constructive tasks. If Christian dogma can be expected to exercise any influence on events, the influence can only be of a magical or theurgic kind. As many Marxists see them, Christians are "practical" people who are very careful not to build their lives on the "utopia" of the beatitudes, although they continue to pay the latter an almost idolatrous worship.

"CHRISTIANITY IS IN A STATE OF DECADENCE; NOTHING IS LEFT OF IT BUT ITS EMPTY FORMS"

René-Marill Albérès, adopting a neutral stance as neither Marxist nor Christian, has analyzed what he calls the "revolt of contemporary writers." Paradoxical though it may seem, he finds the same reasons for revolt operative in both atheistic and believing writers.

For all these writers, whether atheists or Christians, even though they continue to be opposed in language and metaphysics. . . , there is but one enemy to be conquered, one enemy who stands in the way of their mission of bringing light and their desire to confront the problems of the human condition. That enemy is bad faith, posturing, social and intellectual humbug.[6]

Even the militant atheism that shows up in a great deal of contemporary literature (Marxist or nihilist in outlook) is regarded by Albérès as being not a denial of the extramental, objectively existing God (we might say the "Thou" of Marcel or Buber) but a rejection of the gods society has made for itself.

This Promethean revolt is not directed so much against the God of the philosophers and theologians or against his evident absence or the lack of faith in him, as against the divinities that show their face in society. Our modern Prometheus does not rise up against the God of metaphysics and the religions, but against the gods of society.[7]

The Marxist sociologists therefore predict that religion, and chiefly Christianity, will disappear in the near future. Christianity is merely a social mask and will vanish as soon as it is no longer required for justifying decrepit structures that continue to exist—but only as strengthless shadows.

Religion still claims a majority of people around the world, but it stands now for the old. The new, that which is growing and advancing, is atheism. The various Churches recognize this fact; one French prelate recently declared that atheism has now become a fearful mass phenomenon. . . . The decadence of religion will increase as humankind gains a conscious collective control of its own history. Religious conviction may seem to be alive and yet, in fact, be dead. How many believers have stopped believing in God and not realized it? Nothing may have changed in the ritual of worship, but the latter is now only an outward imitation of faith, a purely customary system. Under the influence of social pressure or simply by force of inertia the past continues to assert itself, but it has lost all substance.

Feuerbach had already observed this about Christianity, back in the nineteenth century: "Christianity is rejected, and rejected by those who present themselves as its defenders; the latter do not dare say aloud that they reject it. For political reasons they will not admit it; they keep their rejection secret. The very rejection of Christianity thus passes for Christianity, and Christianity becomes an empty name." Is this not even more true in our own time, especially where Christianity is acclaimed as the dominant ideology? Is it accidental that the societies that most ostentatiously call themselves Christian (Spain and Portugal, for example) are but poor caricatures of the principles they loudly support? Indifference permeates religion from every side. "In the development of law, as in the development of religion," Marx observed, "form replaces substance." Religious behavior, in many believers, is but a surface with nothing behind it.[8]

When confronted with such a serious sociological analysis of a state of affairs that is unfortunately common among Christians, we are forced to reflect anew on our attack on the atheism of those we had been thinking of as having nothing in common with us. An examination of conscience made in the peace of a spiritual retreat does not see atheism as an easy and dangerous temptation for a militant Christianity! Yet we must say that it is in fact the number one temptation. We are in serious danger of falling into a camouflaged atheism such as made Nietzsche say: "I did not elaborate a plan to kill God; I found him dead in the soul of my age."

We have made God part of our hypocritical humbug and crowned him king of a wholly pharisaical society. Then when the pseudovalues of this pharisaical society crumble, as inevitably they must, the false god that provided them with support vanishes in thin air before the eyes of its frightened and astonished worshippers.

Marxist antitheism, with its conscious basis in an economic infrastructure, has an easy time of it in this conjuncture, for, as Bernanos says in his *Lettre aux Anglais:* "What stirs people to revolt in our system is not the material power of money, but the fact that money is regarded not as a tyrant but as a legitimate and honored master whom everyone blesses."

A serious sense of Christian responsibility, therefore, obliges us to turn many of our objections to atheism back upon ourselves and sincerely to revise our own outlook in the light of them.

"RELIGIOUS LOVE IS AN ABSTRACT, ANGELISTIC PSEUDOLOVE"

A reading of the works of Albert Camus, who stood neutral between Marxism and Christianity, is a fine starting point for Christian reflection on the crucial matter of that love for others which Marxist writers claim we Christians lack.

From *The Wedding Feast* to *The Stranger,* from *The Myth of Sisyphus* to *The Rebel,* from *The Plague* to *The Fall,* Camus's main concern has undoubtedly been the problem of happiness. Unlike other philosophers, this writer has no liking for abstract ideas. He was a man who asked penetrating questions about the meaning of the human adventure and was keenly aware of the contradictions that mark life.

He was ever astonished at the beauty of life, but he also suffered from its cruelty. Human well-being was his aim, and he never ceased to stand up against oppression, slavery, and murder, whether during the Spanish War or the German occupation or under Nazism or Communism. He struggled against despair and thought that he had found a way out of sterile, barbarous revolt; but he also wanted to show this way to others, for he considered the human soul to be naturally ordered to its fellows and had within himself that felt need for expression that makes the good writer.

His ambition was to have a clear vision of certain basic realities that ought to mark life: the beauty of the world, the fight against irrational misfortune, solidarity among people. On the supposition that through the centuries rebellion had almost always turned into murderous rage, he thought that philosophy ought, after so many millennia, to provide people with a wisdom that would invite them to collaborate in lessening the evils that afflict them. His was a morality of unity for the sake of understanding; a morality of self-surrender and intelligent action; a morality, in the last analysis, of love, a love that evidently included justice as a basic condition of its sincerity and effectiveness.

In *The Rebel* there is a luminous passage in which the primordial intuition behind Camus's whole outlook finds clear expression; it is the passage in which he defines evil as that which hides people from each other.

It seems at first sight incomprehensible that Camus, though he lived within a Christian society and was penetrated by that ancient Western culture that regards itself as fundamentally Christian, nonetheless had to discover for himself the thing that energizes all Christian action: love of neighbor.

This same state of affairs may explain the fact—hard for us to swallow, but very real—that Marxists have been able to rebuke Christians for "not having loved enough."

Spiritual love does not extend sufficiently to the body and the world so that it can be comfortable with action. An abstract love can only love abstractions. Religious love is limited to love of the soul and thus separates, in its realm of abstractions, things which reality unites in an indissoluble way: "body and soul." It considers "the soul to be holy and the body profane" and thus effects "an unqualified reduction of man to his spiritual ego" (Marx). The pastor, for example, "distinguishes between the criminal and his soul. What he wants to save is not the man, who is the real criminal, but only the criminal's soul." To sustain a love for such an abstraction, abstract means are enough: confession, remorse, and absolution, for example.

But confession will not change the crime committed nor absolution the objective content of the criminal's life. Pardon of the crime does not bring the victim back to life, nor does it put an end to prisons, courts, or the underworld. The evil remains untouched. What the atheist's morality objects to in religious love is not that it loves. The objection is that it has not loved enough! For it has not raised love to the level of a practical truth. On the other hand, the blame can be more justly directed at history. For the impotence of spiritual love simply reflects a great drama being played out through time. If love is to be given universal dimensions *in a practical way,* then it must embody itself in social action. Or, more precisely, in political action, for only the state can effectively give social action universal scope in a class society.

Here is where we run into a dilemma: Either love shuns the political order and falls into an impotent angelism (pure—but without hands!), or else it involves itself in the political order and thereby accepts all the necessities inherent in the use of power. In a sense, however, the dilemma is an illusion. Angelism flees violence, but it does not escape it, for in refusing to use political means all it does is sanction the politics that now holds sway. Thus it becomes an accomplice not only in the violence used by the established state but also in the social violence on which this state is founded: exploitation, colonialism, war, etc.

Angelism is thus impure, even if it doesn't realize the fact. It does not dare take sides with the executioners, but neither does it venture to fight alongside the victims. Two cowardices do not add up to one purity! On the other hand, angelism cannot assure the salvation even of the individual. Even if we assume that it purifies him, it still leaves the collective stain untouched. But of what use is the restless chastity of this or that individual when compared with the enormous collective sin of prostitution? Or the scrupulous refusal to eat meat on Friday when confronted with colonial wars? In the face of evils so vast, even the greatest angels are dwarfs. Religious love is just not big enough.[9]

Here, once again, we are faced with a Marxist rebuke that is based on observation of a sociological phenomenon whose presence in many so-called Christian societies cannot be denied.

It is beyond doubt that the structures of communities that claim to be Christian are not based in a constitutive way on the New Commandment. If fraternal love were truly the motivating power in a society, it would inevitably lead to a greater sharing of the masses in the goods meant for the use of all. Since this does not happen, we must be sincere enough to admit that we are guilty of sacrilege in having put a Christian label on social structures that are really based on the old law of antihuman selfishness.

Nor is it enough to have sprinkled this society with holy water and perfumed it with incense, to have provided a respected place apart in it for ministers of worship, or to have proclaimed its consecration to Christ in solemn, moving acts.

As long as the brotherly love that Christ preached is not the vital force in a society's life, there may be Christians in that society, but the society itself will continue to be pagan, no matter how many Christian labels we stick on it.

"HISTORY WILL DECIDE WHO IS RIGHT"

People have always wanted to work out a philosophy of history that would enable them to control future events with the same degree of certainty as they can now send our fearful modern instruments of destruction to distant targets.

The most recent philosophy of this kind, one of enormous scope, comes from Marxism; it is a philosophy that we have no intention of playing down. Marxism believes that it has found the ultimate key to the course of history, and it uses this as the basis for scientific prophecies.

Religion can hardly hope to survive in a communist society except in some individuals. The vicissitudes of life and the lack of education and culture can always condemn this or that individual to sorrow and misfortune; a life that is not mastered is always fertile ground for a religious sensibility. Those who do not know how to live and conquer and love by their own native powers will perhaps always be tempted to adore God, Fate, or Love (all with upper-case initials!). This is what will happen to the extent that society has seriously failed, in regard to these people, in its duty of educating and giving humane help. But even in these instances what we will see is religious behavior rather than religion in the proper sense. The behavior will increasingly be classified as a pathological exception, somewhat as the practice of magic is in our own time. Marxists, at any rate, think that this is what the future holds. History will decide whether or not they are right.[10]

History here becomes the final court of appeal. Believers and atheists must all some day appear before her judgment seat, and she will utter from her divine mouth an infallible judgment. She will condemn forever the poor fools who thought they could be greater than they were and objectified their dream in the form of a transcendent God.

We Christians too have a final court of appeal, but it consists in the fact that the Son of man shows a supreme indifference to what is great in the eyes of history but is passionately interested in each individual. Christ stoops to the one who is alone with his hidden tragedies and wretched fate; he is interested in each person's concrete, private history. The only criterion Christ will apply is "Did you or did you not serve me in my brothers?" The denouement of the vast drama of history will be wholly surprising, even for the elect.

To sum up: The serious objections raised by Marxism oblige us radically to revise our own theological thinking. As we shall see, the reproaches are generally valid as sociological analyses of the scandalous phenomena to be found in many Christian societies and institutions. We too shall analyze our "Christian" conduct, but in the light of the essential message of salvation, especially as we see it in action in Christianity's founder, Jesus Christ, and find it given doctrinal expression in the writings of the New Testament, Paul in particular.

The French Marxist philosopher Henri Lefèbvre acknowledges that only Christianity, as a vision of the person and the world, can surpass Marxism; but in the Christian theology that he examines from this point of view he does not find the possibility anywhere near realization.

Those opposed to Marxism have today abandoned the effort to refute it piece by piece, fragment by fragment. Their current aim is *to go beyond Marxism.* This means, first of all, that the time of partial polemics is now past. The thing to be subjected to criticism is Marxism as a whole, Marxism as a world view. But what is meant by going beyond, or over-coming, Marxism? Formulas are not enough! Effective action is what is needed. And where are we to find the world view that will overcome the Marxist view? It is nowhere to be seen! Only the Christian view of reality as a whole has sufficient scope to be able to meet Marxism on the doctrinal level, but it is not at all clear why, how, and in what respect Thomism is superior to Marxism.[11]

Our reflections on the message of Christ as it concerns human development represent a modest effort to get back to the sources. We live in an age in which the desire to be original has become a daily obsession. Perhaps this is due to the critical nature of the moment in which we must live our lives, for we are at the point at which two eras meet. The difficult and painful transition between two eras was in earlier times a slow accomplishment and took one or more generations, but today it is happening much more sud-denly and giving rise to a confrontation between two totally diverse conceptions of human development.

For this reason the rising generation feels the need to create, to break with the past, and to say what has never been said before, or at least to say things in a wholly new way. For this reason they regard originality as a highly important human value.

We Christians too have seriously raised the question of the originality of our faith. Is that faith adequate to the needs of the new person who is coming to birth in our time? Marxism, as high priest of the new humankind, has objected that Christianity has now accomplished its mission and has reached the age of retire-ment. It must give way to a new philosophy of humankind, a philosophy that can meet the needs of the new person who walks in the direction history points out to him.

This is the reason many Christians, including professional

theologians, have attempted to create from scratch an "original," wholly new vision of the person and the world. But the product of this hasty adaptation has been an unassimilated mass of ideas that has not only roused justified suspicion or even been condemned by those responsible for doctrine in the Church, but has also been rightly rejected or scorned by Marxist philosophers.

Christianity is not a humanism, that is, it does not present itself as a technique for humanization that is better than comparable techniques. Christianity is a faith in a God who freely gives himself. Consequently, we must attach the label of Pelagianism or Semipelagianism to many theological enterprises that act as though the word of God contained the key to the immanent solution of the problems affecting the person and the world.

Let me repeat what I indicated in the Introduction: Christianity is Marxism's rival, not when the latter is taken as a science or technique for changing society, but when it is taken as a working hypothesis, a philosophical vision of the world, or, if you wish, a specific faith in humankind and its future.

NOTES

1. Ludwig Feuerbach, *The Essence of Christianity,* trans. George Eliot (New York: Harper Torchbook, 1957), p. 14.

2. Karl Marx, "Contribution to the Critique of Hegel's Philosophy of Right," in *Karl Marx: Early Writings,* ed. and trans. T. B. Bottomore (New York: McGraw-Hill, 1963), pp. 43–44.

3. V. I. Lenin, *Sulla religione* (Rome: Rinascite, 1950), pp. 25–26 [Eng. trans.: *On Religion,* 3rd rev. ed. (Moscow: Progress Publishers, 1969)].

4. Ibid., pp. 13–14.

5. Henri Lefèbvre, *Le marxisme,* 15th ed. (Paris: Presses Universitaires de France, 1972).

6. René-Marill Albérès, *La rebelión de los escritores de hoy* [La revolte des écrivains d'aujourd'hui (Paris: Correa, 1949)].

7. Ibid.

8. Michel Verret, *Les marxistes et la religion: Essai sur l'athéisme moderne* (Paris: Editions Sociales, 1961), pp. 178, 182–83.

9. Ibid., pp. 148–50.

10. Ibid., p. 211.

11. Lefèbvre, *Le marxisme.*

CHAPTER 2

THE PURPOSE OF HUMAN EFFORT

If we were to attempt to sum up the problem of the human condition in one key statement, we might say that it boils down to the search for a satisfactory meaning for the efforts the person expends in trying to shape his life within the context of space and time. Every person wants to "live his life." He wants, that is, to develop himself so as to reach an objective that will fully satisfy him. The person produces things and gives a shape to himself, but to what end?

Christianity, as we shall see, is essentially an adequate response to this anxious human question. But first we shall review, even if only in a broad and undetailed way, the two most important responses that have been given to this question in addition to the Christian response. These two responses are still influential today and even intrude themselves into the very responses given from a supposedly Christian point of view.

"HUMAN EFFORT IS DIRECTED TO THE FORMATION OF THE PERSON AS A SPECIES-BEING"

This is the Marxist answer. Marxism aims at a complete reconciliation between person and person and between person and nature, but the subject of reconciliation is not really the individual; it is the species.

The person here is what Marx calls, in his *Theses on Feuerbach*, ''a species-being,'' that is, a being who ''treats himself as the present, living species.''[1]

Species-life, for man as for animals, has its physical basis in the fact that man (like animals) lives from inorganic nature. . . . Nature is the inorganic body of man; that is to say nature, excluding the human body itself. To say that man *lives* from nature means that nature is his *body* with which he must remain in a continuous interchange in order not to die. The statement that the physical and mental life of man, and nature, are interdependent means simply that nature is interdependent with itself, for man is a part of nature.[2]

For Marxism, then, the person becomes of interest only when viewed at the level of the species. The human species is both nature and society—a society that has its foundations in nature, and a nature that unfolds in society. There is, therefore, no problem of the person, but only the problem of the evolution of society and the determinism of nature.

The point at which this Marxist anthropology falls completely short is in its outlook on death. Verret begins his reflections on death with a poetic exclamation: ''There remains death. Highest hope and highest object of thought for the theologian! Will people ever give up their hope of survival? And if they do not, will that not be enough to leave religion in possession of all its hopes, since religion undertakes to provide assurance of immortality?''[3]

The Marxist explanation of death is intelligible only when the human being is seen as a species-being.

Everything raises in our minds the question of death. But everything also gives us the answer. Question and answer are given us simultaneously by life itself: by our individual lives and by the life of society. The answer is always the same: Death is only a moment, a point, in an ongoing event. More than that, it is the necessary condition of movement and progress, the condition of life itself, for in the ceaseless struggle between contraries death is the way in which the new asserts itself against the old. Every form of existence arises out of another, which it then destroys. The price of spring is the death of winter. Childhood must die if we are to become adults. The meaning of *my* individual death is no different from these other deaths. My death is absurdity and scandal from the viewpoint simply of the individual, but it takes on meaning from the viewpoint of the species. ''The death of the fathers is the life of the sons'' (Hegel). It is in a sense the condition for the succession of generations, for otherwise the earth would be crowded with elderly people. The constant youthfulness of humankind depends on the deaths of individuals. . . .

The exemplary deaths of the martyrs and saints had its deepest motivation in love, and the heroism of many communists was fed from the same source. The working class now practices that same heroism quite naturally, for, as we collectively face the future, the deaths of individuals are clearly part of the onward march of humankind. . . .

Shall our works die? And our children too? Of course, they will. But our children will have children in turn, and our works will have their posterity. "The individual passes, but the species never ends; that is what gives meaning to the individual even though he perishes" (Diderot). . . . The movement of history can sweep me away, and with me my name and my works, and even the very memory that I have lived. But then I survive in a different way, in the very movement that swept me away and negated me, provided I have contributed to creating the conditions needed for change. Such sharing in the process of change becomes, paradoxically, the means of giving me an unending existence. In a sense, only the reactionary wholly dies. The revolutionary, on the contrary, lives again in a small way in all future revolutions. . . . The human story is that of the phoenix: We achieve immortality only by dying.[4]

The worst thing about this outlook is that it not only minimizes the death of the individual but completely denies all meaning to his very existence. The individual really does not exist. Marxism is the throwback to the cloudy collectivism that marks human prehistory, when the greatest effort of humankind for millennia had to be expended in gradually bringing to the light of awareness the individuality of the human person.

The Marxist solution is a purely speculative one, for it is humankind that does not exist; humanity is a pure mental abstraction. What really exists is this person and this one and this one. But none of them can hope to achieve total human fulfillment. For, even if the last generation on earth were to gather to itself the whole immensely rich heritage produced by the efforts of people over millennia of time and were to turn out to be composed of a few quite perfect superbeings, even then the anguish arising from awareness that they too must pass away would detract from their hypothetical fulfillment. The superbeing too must die. Moreover, the sacrifice of these countless millions in past ages would be monstrously disproportionate to such an ephemeral result as one last hyperdeveloped generation.

A further point to be considered is that the Marxist view of the human being as a species-being inevitably leads to the infamous totalitarianisms that enslave immense multitudes of people. Millions are sacrificed on the altar of a voracious Moloch, whose name has ever been "Empire," though various adjectives have preceded the name at various points in history: Egyptian, Roman, Holy, Nazi, Soviet. Perhaps the modern concept of "fatherland" is a holdover from the ancient totalitarians of early history, for "fatherland" has now become one of humankind's widespread myths to which countless hordes of concrete people, real people of flesh and blood, are ruthlessly sacrificed. Perhaps even the concept of the "common good," as sometimes explained in ethical systems of supposedly Christian inspiration, represents the same kind of deadly substitution of the purely imaginary abstract for the concrete existent.

There is another and even more radical consideration that makes the anthropological outlook of Marxism unacceptable. There are moments in life when the extent of human mediocrity and folly stirs feelings of almost metaphysical disgust in us. It seems simply not worthwhile that people and things should continue even to exist. All that is sterile and ineffective and unproductive passes before our eyes as monotonously as a constantly repeated film and dins in our tired ears with the irritating whine of a broken record.

Only from time to time does some interesting character stand out, solitary and impressive. For a moment we feel a new optimism about the human race, but unfortunately the enthusiasm is short-lived. We are confronted once again by endless lines of completely standardized, undifferentiated people.

Marxism does not find this spectacle repulsive. The person is, after all, only a sum total of usable qualities that can be pressed out like juice by the immense wheels of the totalitarian, collectivist machinery. To the Marxist, the human person does not, in practice, exist. Humankind becomes a kind of immense breeding farm where experiments are carried on to determine the best ways of achieving the betterment of the species. If a flower is to blossom, a lot of fertilizer has to be put into the pot. It does not matter how much human fertilizer is used, provided that some extraordinarily endowed geniuses emerge or that Humanity—this abstract, nonexistent collectivity—can be written with an ever larger capital letter.

But even such an explanation in terms of human fertilizer and its use is incomplete and unsatisfactory. For, in cultivating geniuses and improving the species only a small percentage of the human fertilizer is used. To what purpose, then, the immense quantities of pain, helplessness, forced unproductiveness, ignorance, and stupidity that fills the pots in which human existence is continuously coming to birth? What purpose is served by the dead fetuses, the children who die before the age of reason, the mentally defective, the paralytics, the crippled, the leprous, the cancer-ridden, and the aged?

Let us anticipate here what we shall dwell on more fully later in speaking of the Christian response: for Christianity does have an adequate response to this human anguish. It claims that the pain, even if unconscious, of humankind has a beneficent influence on the ascending progress of history toward its fulfillment. More than that—and here is the really new thing Christianity says: All this human fertilizer is not simply used to bring forth a flower or a few flowers; it is itself miraculously recast and transformed into flowers. Every bit of dung, that is, every free, rational person, can be transformed into a person who is whole and perfect.

Faith in the resurrection is the only anthropology worthy of the dignity of the human person.

"HUMAN EFFORT SERVES ONLY TO PREPARE THE SPIRIT TO TAKE FLIGHT"

This is the response given by Greek philosophy and all forms of religious quietism.

In this view, human effort does not have its goal within the limits of the visible cosmos or the existential sphere determined by our bodily condition, but reaches into the invisible world of the spirit or "pneumatosphere." Human effort is therefore not concerned with the progressive transformation of matter, world, and history, but only with acquiring a passport into the supracosmic realm of the spirit. Transformation of the cosmos yields to struggle against the cosmos with the purpose of overcoming its influence and leaving it behind, thus preparing the way for a definitive escape from it and entry into the place of the spirit. In short, human effort is regarded as constructive only insofar as it effects a series of partial escapes from matter and the universe and thus prepares the way for the final complete escape that will completely free us from the burden of the body and all that is part of this universe, and allow it to enter the invisible world of the spirit.

In this Greek conception of human effort the problem of death once again determines the whole perspective that is adopted. The human being, according to the Greek philosophers, is essentially "spirit" or "pneuma." And corresponding to it, there is a "pneumatosphere," in which genuinely existent realities live in the presence of the Supreme Being. Matter belongs to the pseudoworld of nonbeing or less-being.

The human "spirit," however, has been locked in the prison of the body, that is, of matter. The body keeps the spirit from taking flight and reaching its full development. Therefore the person's true goal is to free himself from this hindrance: "The philosopher's occupation consists precisely in the freeing and separation of soul from body."[5]

Death, then, ceases to be the greatest of evils and becomes the greatest of blessings.

True philosophers make dying their profession, and . . . to them of all men death is least alarming. Look at it this way. If they are thoroughly dissatisfied with the body, and long to have their souls independent of it, when this happens would it not be entirely unreasonable to be frightened and distressed? Would they not naturally be glad to set out for the place where there is a prospect of attaining the object of their lifelong desire, which is Wisdom; and of escaping from an unwelcome association?[6]

A logical conclusion from this conception is that death does not mean distance from God, as it does in the Bible, but an approach to the divine, a kind of flight to a sphere where the spirit shares in the vital rhythm of the gods.

If this [purity, etc.] is its [the soul's] condition, then it departs to that place which is, like itself, invisible, divine, immortal and wise; where, on its arrival, happiness awaits it, and release from uncertainty and folly, from fears and uncontrolled desires, and all other human evils; and where (as they say of the initiates in the Mysteries) it really spends the rest of time with God.[7]

After death the person regains his true and complete being. Socrates is convinced of this and therefore quibbles with Crito when the latter asks Socrates how they are to bury *him*. Socrates says they cannot bury him, because he is the soul which at death escapes from empirical reality; the soul is the true person, while the body does not belong in even a secondary way to the essence of the true human being.

You must assure him [Crito] that when I am dead I shall not stay, but depart and be gone. That will help Crito to bear it more easily, and keep him from being distressed on my account when he sees my body being burned or buried, as if something dreadful were happening to me; or from saying at the funeral that it is Socrates whom he is laying out or carrying to the grave or burying. Believe me, my dear friend Crito: misstatements are not merely jarring in their immediate context; they also have a bad effect upon the soul. No, you must keep up your spirits and say that it is only my body that you are burying; and you can bury it as you please, in whatever way you think is most proper.[8]

The death of this great philosopher has in the course of time gotten wrapped in rosy twilight clouds of romantic nostalgia; this has happened precisely because of the great effort he made to answer the supreme question of death, which causes anxiety in the very depths of the human heart. Socrates in fact finds no solution to the problem, and therefore he tries to suppress it. But he is unable to dry the bitter tears of his close friends, immensely human people who cannot resign themselves to looking on the body as something extrinsic to the person.

The Socratic solution to the problem of death never became popular, yet it did succeed in controlling a philosophy of asceticism that would permeate many levels of Western history and leave a profound mark even on many Christian thinkers and ascetics.

To sum up: In this view, human effort is effective and liberating precisely to the extent that it sets itself against the movement of history. The world, matter, time, and space simply provide the context in which the "spirit" exercises its power by overcoming those obstacles formed by matter and the world that would try to keep the spirit in this sphere of nonbeing or less-being. In such a perspective the idea of constructing the world and history is completely without meaning.

"HUMAN EFFORT IS MEANT TO PREPARE THE PERSON NOW FOR THE INDIVIDUAL FULFILLMENT THAT WILL BE ATTAINED IN THE FINAL RESURRECTION"

The Christian response to the anguished human question about death is given within a strictly biblical perspective according to which the body is essential to the person and death is an evil, indeed something so terrible that God did not want it and in a way it keeps us from nearness to God.

Oscar Cullmann has splendidly contrasted for us the death of Socrates and the death of Jesus. The two events are the focal points of irreconcilable views of life.[9]

We have just seen how Socrates confronted death with immense peace, for death was his sweet friend. His death was a beautiful death, completely without any touch of horror; he did not fear dying, for to die was to be freed from the body.

Let us now turn to quite a different scene, the last hours of Jesus. In Gethsemane Jesus knew very clearly that death was waiting for him, no less than Socrates knew it when he carried on his last conversation with his friends. But, unlike Socrates, Jesus "began to be filled with fear and distress" (Mark 14:34). Jesus is so completely human that he shares the inborn fear that death arouses in us all. He is not a coward who fears the people who will execute him nor the suffering that will precede death. What he fears is death itself, that terribly powerful hold that evil has upon humankind. For Jesus, death is not something divine, but something to rouse horror. He really trembles before this great enemy of God. There is nothing here of Socrates' serenity as he goes calmly to his death as to a great friend. Instead, Jesus prays that God save him from the awful moment. He already knows, of course, that the task entrusted to him is precisely to die; he had said earlier: "I have a baptism to receive. What anguish I feel till it is over!" (Luke 12:50). But now that the enemy of God is upon him, he prays to the Father whose omnipotence he knows: "You have the power to do all things. Take this cup away from me" (Mark 14:36). And when he adds, "But let it be as you would have it, not as I," the meaning is not that in the last analysis he, like Socrates, regards death as a liberating friend. No! The meaning is simply: If it be your will that this terrible thing, death, have its way with me, I submit to its horror.

The Epistle to the Hebrews, which more than any other New Testament writing stresses both the full divinity (Heb. 1:10) and the humanity of Jesus, goes even further than the three synoptic narratives in its description of Jesus' anguish in the face of death. "He offered prayers and supplications with loud cries and tears to God, who was able to save him from death" (5:7).

Finally, as death becomes imminent, the contrast between the two outlooks becomes even clearer. With sovereign calm and self-control Socrates drains the cup of hemlock. Jesus, on the contrary, cries out in the words of the Psalmist: "My God, my God, why have you forsaken me?" and then, uttering an inarticulate cry, dies (Mark 15:34, 37). This is not the death that is our friend but death in all its naked horror, death the "last enemy" of God, as Paul calls it (1 Cor. 15:26). In this phrase we can see the abysmal difference between Greek thought on the one side and the Jewish and Christian faith on the other. The Apocalypse uses different language but it too regards death as the last enemy, as it describes how at the end death will be hurled into the pool of fire (Rev. 20:14).

Since death is God's enemy it separates us from him who is *life and the creator of all life.* It follows that since Jesus is completely in union with God, more so than any other human being can ever be (since he himself is God), death must be more repugnant to him than to any other person. He must experience this isolation and separation from God (in the last analysis this is the *only situation* that really deserves to be feared) infinitely more intensely than others, precisely because he is so closely united to God. This is why he calls out to God with the Psalmist: "Why have you forsaken me?" In this final moment of life he is really in the hands of God's great enemy, death. We must pay tribute to the evangelist for not softening the details of his description.

The same outlook on death and life permeates the whole Bible, and we must grasp it fully if we are fully to understand the Christian response to the question of the ultimate meaning to be given to human effort.

The Bible keeps in mind both dimensions of the human tragedy, so much so that the two seem at times almost to become identified: The human being is wretched both physically and morally. His physical wretchedness takes shape in the way of pain that begins with the first cries of the newborn child and ends in the fearful and horrible thing we call death.

His moral wretchedness consists of sin. But sin has a somewhat different meaning for the biblical writers than it does for the West. To the Roman (who set the tone for the West) sin is identifiable with guilt in the moral sense of this word as applied to the individual. In the Bible sin is a much more inclusive concept: It is something that enfolds the person like an atmosphere, so that there can be a kind of objective sin that is even independent of the free choice of the individual; thus there are sins of error or of inadvertence.[10]

For this reason, throughout biblical thought death is a religious concept that becomes almost identical with sin. Both death and sin are forms of separation from God. God is life; death is remoteness from life and therefore from God. Consequently, too, we find throughout the Old Testament a close connection between the two pairs, death-sin and life-virtue. The person who obeys the commandments of God is on the path of life; the person who is unfaithful to God's law is on the path of death. "Here, then, I have today set before you life and prosperity, death and doom. If you obey the commandments of the Lord, your God, which I enjoin on you today, loving him, . . . you will live and grow numerous, and the Lord, your God, will bless you. . . . For that will mean life for you, a long life" (Deut. 30:15–20).[11]

In order, then, properly to evaluate the biblical teaching on sin and death and the mutual relations between them, we must bear in mind this concrete, historical outlook and not project into the sacred text our own sharply defined and extensively explicated philosophical concepts.

Death, for the Old Testament, was something God had not wanted; as a matter of historical fact it had caused separation from God and enmity toward him. Death would always be the great enemy of God (cf. 1 Cor. 15:26). It symbolizes the collapse of that beautiful architecture of creation which the Yahwist writer describes for us in such optimistic terms at the beginning of Genesis.

Given this perspective, we can understand that for an Israelite the proclamation of redemption or liberation from this state of sin must necessarily bring with it the definitive defeat of death and the unconditional victory of life.

When Paul, in his Epistle to the Romans, presents a complete theology of human fulfillment, he makes his own this unambiguous perspective of the Old Testament. The first part of the letter (chapters one to eight) develops in a coherent and harmonious way the thesis that the human being is wretched, doomed to death and inescapably trapped by countless alienating forces that prevent him from being his true self.

In our own times Marxist anthropology has tackled the same problem and in almost identical terms: the points of departure in both anthropologies are similar, but the paths laid out and the goals are radically distinct, as we shall see.

Paul is a thorough realist and acknowledges the saddening fact of the weakness that causes so much anguish: "What a wretched man I am! Who can free me from this body under the power of death?" (Rom. 7:24).

If we are properly to understand Paul's whole thought in the first part of the letter, it is important to bear in mind the close connection in his thinking between the terms of these two pairs: *sin-death* and *justification-life*.

The human being is in a state of alienation; that is, concretely, he is a being-for-death, not because this was his original destiny according to the Creator's plan, but because at the very beginning of his existence he committed a first sin that cut him off from the sources of life. He was created by God for life in the full sense of this term, but his rebellion against the Creator brought upon him the just anger of God. From that point on and for that reason the person is now mortal and subject to countless anxieties and sorrows.

God, however, had compassion on his creature and determined to restore him from his tragic condition. Such a rescue must necessarily have two aspects: liberation from sin and liberation from death.

In the fifth chapter of his letter Paul paints a splendid picture with two panels on which the parallel but inverse paths are shown which lead from sin to death, on the one hand, and from justification to life, on the other. Through the action of a single man sin entered the world and through sin death; both sin and death have, in a mysterious fashion, infected the whole of the human race. However, when the moment of redemption came, through the activity of a single man, Christ, justification was effected, and with it reconciliation with God and the restoration of life through the sure hope of resurrection.

The later influence of a Platonic anthropology that regarded the body as an extrinsic appendage to the person (the person himself being a pure spirit) obscured somewhat the Pauline vision that was in itself so clearly presented. When Paul speaks of "life," he does not use the word in a purely "spiritual" sense; that is, he does not take "life" as a simple equivalent of reconciliation with God or justification or grace. For him life means the absence of death, the restoration of the body in the form of a glorified body that is forever liberated from all weakness. It is what we today so often call "spiritual life" that Paul identifies with justification, reconciliation, and grace.

Here then is the Apostle's splendid vision. Today, when the Church is already a tangible reality and the Holy Spirit is visibly poured out upon the faithful, we are sure that the first part of the redemptive plan has been carried out: We are justified and reconciled with God.

This reconciliation is God's work and pure gift. The human person was radically incapable of achieving reconciliation with God by his own powers and resources. He had to cast aside any trust in himself and entrust himself solely to God from whom he would hope for everything.

Faith was the only way to lay hold of the redemption that God freely and generously offers us through Jesus Christ. Of course, once possessed, this faith had to be translated into positive good works, and Paul lays heavy stress on this, even specifying what fruits the spiritual life ought to yield in the moral order.

Now—argues Paul—if the infinite step from sin to justification is a tangible fact, how can anyone doubt the future reality of the final leap from justification to life in the resurrection? On a day-to-day basis the Christian is not evidently distinguished from the non-Christian, both being subjected to the greatest of alienations, death. Yet the death of the Christian is in fact a special death, since in baptism he has already been incorporated into the death of Christ. The effective significance of this is that the Christian's death is not an end, but a seed springing up into resurrection. "Are you not aware that we who are baptized into Christ Jesus were baptized into his death? Through baptism into his death we were buried with him, so that, just as Christ was raised from the dead by the glory of the Father, we too might live a new life" (Rom. 6:3–4).

The Christian therefore dies, not his own hopeless and irreversible death, but the death of Christ, a death from which he passes over to life and resurrection.

Paul does not offer a purely spiritual compensation (spiritual in the modern sense of the word) to the person who is deeply distressed by the pain and death he must suffer. On the contrary, he promises a total liberation, a complete cessation of pain and death. First, a person must accept the reconciliation God freely offers him through the mediation of Christ and his Church. But this reconciliation is a sure pledge that, even though we must pass through the dark tunnel of death, a glorious radiant life awaits us in a beyond that is real and concrete and where the risen and glorified Christ, head of the new race, is already living a life that will never end.

The task of the Church is to continue sowing throughout the present creation the seeds of glory that will prepare creation for the unveiling of its true being in a stable and definitive situation. "We know that all creation groans and is in agony even until now. Not only that, but we ourselves, although we have the Spirit as first fruits, groan inwardly while we await the redemption of our bodies" (Rom. 8:22–23).

Here we have the most important point on which Paul and Marx are in agreement. At the same time, however, it is here that both thinkers begin to open up perspectives that will lead them ever farther apart. Both agree that humankind has a history and that the history has a rhythm. This rhythm, even while it is now being deflected and obscured by alienations and absurdity, must be directed by a powerful hand toward the true goal. That goal is the creation of a new person.

But Marx's person is a ''species-being''; in Marx's view liberation is not promised to the individual. Humankind, however, will reach a better state when his economic difficulties have been resolved.

Marx himself in all his writings devotes but a single sentence to the greatest of alienations, death. He acknowledges the fact of death but immediately tries to push it aside, thus declaring that he is powerless to deal with it. *"Death* seems to be a harsh victory of the species over the individual and to contradict their unity; but the particular individual is only a *determinate species-being* and as such he is mortal.''[12]

For Paul, however, the goal of humankind is not the species-being but the concrete Person, Jesus Christ, who is the New Adam, the new and final Person. The task of the Church is to incorporate the individual person into the sphere of Christ's saving power. Such action on the part of the Church is not purely eschatological nor purely individualistic. It does not consist simply in offering transitory, mortal people the compensation of a spiritual life that is separated from and independent of the body and the world. It consists rather in exerting influence on the body and the world so as gradually to prepare them for their final and definitive goal: ''the glorious freedom of the children of God'' (Rom. 8:21).

The new people of God, for which Paul is drawing up the charter in his Epistle to the Romans, has a mission in this world. This people becomes reality within the history of humankind and continuously sows there the seeds that will someday bear fruit in the ''new heavens and. . . new earth where, according to his promise, the justice of God will reside'' (2 Pet. 3:13).

Paul, a man who has his feet solidly on the ground, has very concrete plans for the carrying out of this long-range mission. He sees quite clearly the realities of life in the time in which he lives and realizes therefore that Rome affords an ideal center from which effectively to bring to the world the seed of immortality that will one day yield the fruit of eternal glory.

The recent nineteen-hundredth anniversary commemoration of the Epistle to the Romans provides a very suitable occasion for us Christians to examine our consciences with regard to the great sin we have committed in modern times by absenting ourselves from the movement of world history. We have turned in on ourselves; we have fixed our eyes on a purely spiritual beyond; influenced by a false asceticism that arises out of cowardice and laziness, we have dispensed ourselves from stooping down to the proletarian who lies in the gutters of our streets and have, instead, gone our way proud and unconcerned, attentive only to the elegant sacred fillets that crown our priestly or levitical heads.

We have forgotten the very heart of the Pauline message concerning the Church's mission. The Church's function is not simply to build itself up and to make itself the center and goal of its own growth. It is rather to grow ever stronger so that it may better carry out its mission of saving everything and bringing the world to its ultimate fulfillment.

Some day, *this world*—the world in which sin and its offspring, physical and moral evil, hold sway—will become the *other world,* the future world, the kingdom of God. But the passage from the one to the other will not be effected by a divine decree that is wholly extrinsic to the development of the world itself in which we live. The transition will be a slow one that takes place through the course of history. History will be progressively enlightened and become filled with the light of Christ until the darkness gradually disappears. The task of effecting this illumination is the mission proper to the Church.

Sin was the standard-bearer for all the calamities that have fallen upon humankind. The Church's task is to dislodge sin from the positions it has conquered. But in the present order of things sin is also closely connected with all the other evils that afflict us. Consequently, the Church must also work for the elimination of these evils as well.

The beneficent action of the Church is not something secondary nor something added on to its religious function. On the contrary, it is at the very heart of the mission proper to it. We Christians must work hard in dealing with the matter and the spirits that constitute the world and in trying to elevate them within their own proper order and to apply to them the anointing of Christ. We cannot fold our arms and raise our eyes to a hypothetical heaven that is but the child of our own imagination, in hopes that the salvation of the world will be sent down to us ready-made.

To sum up: Human effort will someday reach its terminus. Then human fulfillment will flow out upon each and every person, from the mythical person of five hundred thousand years ago to the hypercivilized individual of the last generation on earth. What people are promised is resurrection, which means the definitive transition to a fully human life that knows no shadow or threat, no lack or defect.

The human effort expended through the millennia will not have been in vain, for it will have contributed to the maturation of humankind and thus brought it to the utmost boundaries of fulfillment.

At a certain moment God himself broke into human history and called himself Jesus of Nazareth, who was a complete person with all that this entailed. Jesus lived a life like everyone else and died the death that all must die. But he returned immediately from the realm of death and manifested himself as filled with a life that could never again be lost. He became the pioneer leader of the human race and took his place as Lord of creation.

We now know that it is possible to emerge from death. But the efforts of people through the millennia have not succeeded in attaining their objective, although they have not therefore been ineffective or in vain. Jesus came to gather up the efforts expended in the old world and to give them new vigor, thus inserting a new and efficacious impulse into the secular work of humankind.

The impulse in question is the life-giving breath of love, universal brotherly love. And once this enormous force is largely commanded and directed by Christian love, humankind will be very close to its final moment of definitive maturity. Christ will return as he promised; he will consider the enterprise of human development as completed and will bestow upon us his own life in all its plenitude and invulnerability.

That such a high value is to be set upon human effort even in its material and secular forms follows from that great saving event that is the essence of Christianity. Paul says that at a predetermined moment in the course of time "God sent forth his Son born of a woman, born under the law" (Gal. 4:4). Christ was not a kind of heavenly body lowered from the sky but a natural product of the long evolution of human life. His birth indeed had something marvelous or "miraculous" about it; he nonetheless came forth from the womb of history and was wholly a piece with it.

The incarnation of Christ is not a divine pretense or masquerade, after the fashion of what we read in the marvel-filled narratives of the Greek and Roman poets. Christ was not a god who condescended to play the part of a sublime protagonist on the world's great stage. He was a real person and a complete person. His reactions were spontaneous; his laughter and tears sprang, like vital energies, from a nature rich in experience and sensitivity.

If Jesus Christ is in any way different from other mortals, it is—paradoxical though this may sound—in his attachment to life. He called himself "the life" (John 14:6). "I came that they might have life and have it to the full" (John 10:10). Christ loved life as no other person has ever loved it. His incarnation—better, his hominization—was to be permanent. Because of him death would be stripped of its finality and become a temporary, provisional state. Thus the seal of completion is placed on Christ's incarnation by his resurrection. From that moment on, God has committed himself for good to matter and the cosmos.

Christ and Mary, now definitively restored to life through resurrection, are the anticipatory first fruits of the coming apotheosis of matter. They are the most *real* beings in the entire creation, as well as the beings most fully immersed in and committed to matter.

For this reason, and with no intention of being paradoxical, we can rightly say that Christianity is a religion which is essentially, even if not exclusively, materialist. Forgetfulness of this deeply material aspect of our religion is the reason why Christianity has been accused of what is the very opposite of the truth: the absence of matter.

We must observe that Marx, like Feuerbach and Nietzsche, constantly confuses Christianity with its opposite, the Manichean heresy. When he blames Christianity for teaching that "matter is infected with original sin," he is addressing himself to the wrong party. What even today repels the best and most demanding of the pagans who are far from Christianity is in fact the elements of Manicheanism still to be found in Christianity.[13]

Catholic theology expresses in a lapidary axiom the truth of which we are here speaking: "Whatever [including matter] God has once assumed he will never set aside."

NOTES

1. The second quotation is from "Alienated Labour," a section of the first of the "Economic and Philosophical Manuscripts (1844)," in *Karl Marx: Early Writings*, p. 126. The term "species-being" is not synonymous with "the abstract human being." "When Marx says that the subject of history cannot be the abstract or 'imaginary' person but only the active, real person, the person as producer, he reminds us of what is basic not only from the historical and social points of view but also for understanding the person anthropologically and psychologically" (C. I. Gouliane, *Le marxisme devant l'homme* [Paris: Payot, 1968], p. 30). Cf. *Karl Marx: Early Writings*, p. 13, n. 2: "The terms 'species-life' (*Gattungsleben*) and 'species-being' (*Gattungswesen*) are derived from Feuerbach. In the first chapter of *Das Wesen des Christentums* [*The Essence of Christianity*], Leipzig, 1841, Feuerbach discusses the nature of man, and argues that man is to be distinguished from animals not by 'consciousness' as such, but by a particular kind of consciousness. Man is not only conscious of himself as an individual; he is also conscious of himself as a member of the human species, and so he apprehends a 'human essence' which is the same in himself and in other men. According to Feuerbach this ability to conceive of 'species' is the fundamental element in the human power of reasoning: 'Science is the consciousness of species.' Marx, while not departing from this meaning of the terms, employs them in other contexts; and he insists more strongly than Feuerbach that since this 'species-consciousness' defines the nature of man, man is only living and acting authentically (i.e. in accordance with his nature) when he lives and acts deliberately as a 'species-being,' that is, as a *social* being." —Trans. note.]

2. Marx, "Alienated Labour," *Karl Marx: Early Writings*, pp. 126–27.

3. Verret, *Marxistes et religion*, p. 160.

4. Ibid., pp. 168–72.

5. Plato, "Phaedo," 67d, trans. Hugh Tredennick, *The Last Days of Socrates (Euthyphro, Apology, Crito, Phaedo)* (Baltimore: Penguin, 1954), p. 113.

6. Ibid., 67e–68a, p. 113.

7. Ibid., 81a, p. 133.

8. Ibid., 115d–e, p. 180.

9. Oscar Cullmann, *Immortality of the Soul or Resurrection of the Dead? The Witness of the New Testament* (London: Epworth, 1958). The next five paragraphs

of our text are a summary, using Cullmann's own language, of pp. 21–25 of his little book.

10. Cf. Num. 15:27; Lev. 4:2, 27; Gen. 50:5; 2 Sam. 5:4–7; Num. 22:32.

11. Cf. Deut. 32:47; 28:1–14; Ps. 37:9–10; Prov. 3:1–10.

12. Marx, ''Economic and Philosophical Manuscripts (1844),'' In *Karl Marx: Early Writings,* pp. 158–59.

13. Claude Tresmontant, *Estudios de metafísica bíblica* (Madrid: Gredos, 1961), p. 227.

CHAPTER 3

THE GOD OF CHRISTIAN FAITH

GOD HAS BEEN KILLED!

It is almost a century now since Nietzsche put on a madman's lips the chilling words: "God is dead!" More exactly: People have killed God. The exclamation was not uttered by laughing drunkards; it rose from the depths of anguished wonder and astonishment.

Since that time the Nietzschean cry has achieved a fearful popularity through the powerful tools of modern technology. Militant atheism has won over to its cause a third of the earth's inhabitants. A devastating humanism makes it a condition of human happiness that the corpse of God be totally destroyed, since its stench still contaminates the two-thirds of the human race that still lives in humiliation and degradation.

What has happened? Some sixteen centuries ago, a great thinker—perhaps the greatest in history—experienced the vertigo that the temptation to slay God can cause in the human heart. Augustine was walking along the Mediterranean seashore trying to grasp with his powerful mind the infinite God. He came across a child playing in the sand and attempting to enclose the immense sea in the poor little hollow his hands had scooped out. Seeing him, Augustine understood his own rashness; he stopped thinking of God as "he" and henceforth dealt with him always as "thou," as a being who confronts us and is superior to us. His magnificent *Confessions* are an ongoing dialogue between "I" and "thou."

But Nietzsche was right to some extent. People have sought to kill God. They have stopped thinking of God as an absolute, transcendent Thou and made of him an idea cut to the measure of the human mind. God has been tailored to fit within the boundaries of human thought and judgment. He has been reduced to an idea and a feeling; it is as if we were to reduce the sun to a mere sensation of light and heat. The result has been an eclipse.

Then one day that proud human being who could not bend his knee and humble himself before the divine Thou began fearfully to observe that his mind and sensibility were giving off a foul, corrupt odor, and he realized that he could not digest the false God he had made for himself. Then he began to look for a cure, for some way of cleansing his system of its intoxication with the ''divine.''

Human refusal of dialogue with God is often reflected in the argument from the presence of pain and evil in the world and especially as these afflict children. With Ivan Karamazov he refuses to accept a world in which children suffer. If God allows such suffering, he is not good or not omnipotent or not omnipresent, and therefore he is not God. ''The only excuse God has is that he does not exist'' (Stendahl).

As to the pain and cruelty God ''permits,'' it can disprove his existence only on the premise—hardly respectable—that God has the same standards and values as men, by whose measure alone there is cruelty and pain. On the other hand, man's rebellion against the processes of nature and of human nature by which pain and cruelty come, could be taken as prima facie evidence that man has a standard of judgment transcending empirical nature, including his own nature: a standard which might be said to issue from God within him. To posit a God with human measures and then to abolish him because he does not satisfy these measures is childish.[1]

As we here attempt to engage not in philosophy or even theodicy but in theology with a specifically Christian stamp, we begin to realize that the holy book, the Bible, has taught us dialogue with God. The Bible is God's biography. From it we know his name, his real name as a concrete being. He introduces himself to Moses as ''the God of your father, the God of Abraham, the God of Isaac, the God of Jacob'' (Exod. 3:6). But even this description seems too generic, and therefore God accepts Moses' request and tells him his own private name, the hidden name that differentiates him from all others: He is "I Am" (Exod. 3:14).

The dialogue of God with humankind begins with creation itself. In the splendid hymn of creation that we read in Genesis, when God creates the other things besides man and woman, he speaks of them only in the third person. " 'Let there be lights in the dome of the sky. . . . ' And so it happened. . . . 'Let the water teem with an abundance of living creatures, and on the earth let birds fly beneath the dome of the sky.' And so it happened" (Gen. 1:14–15, 20). There is indeed a moment when God can, as it were, no longer bear his solitude and attempts direct communication with subhuman living things: "Be fertile, multiply, and fill the water of the seas," but then he reverts to the third person: "and let the birds multiply on the earth" (Gen. 1:22).

Dialogue, with all its vitality and dynamism, begins only when the human being issues from the creative hands of God and God makes him his "partner": "God created man in his image; in the divine image he created him; male and female he created them. God blessed them, saying: 'Be fertile and multiply; fill the earth and subdue it' " (Gen. 1:27–28).

The dialogue constantly increases in frequency and scope. God descends to the garden where man and woman live and engages in animated conversation with them. He threatens, chastises, promises, and pardons, always communicating directly with them and seeking a response from them.

It is always God who initiates the dialogue; in the encounter between Creator and creature, God always starts things off. He manifests himself to man, chooses him, exalts him. "It was not because you are the largest of all nations that the Lord set his heart on you and chose you, for you are really the smallest of all nations. It was because the Lord loved you" (Deut. 7:7–8).

Thus says the Lord God to Jerusalem: By origin and birth you are of the land of Canaan; your father was an Amorite and your mother a Hittite. . . . Then I passed by and saw you weltering in your blood. I said to you: Live in your blood and grow like a plant of the field. You grew and developed, you came to the age of puberty; your breasts were formed, your hair had grown, but you were still stark naked. Again I passed by you and saw that you were now old enough for love. So I spread the corner of my cloak over you to cover your nakedness; I swore an oath to you and entered into a covenant with you; you became mine, says the Lord God. Then I bathed you with water, washed away your blood, and anointed you with oil. I clothed you with an embroidered gown, put sandals of fine leather on your feet; I gave you a fine linen sash and silk robes to wear. I adorned you with jewelry, I put bracelets on your arms, a necklace about your neck, a ring in your nose, pendants in your ears, and a glorious diadem upon your head. Thus you were adorned with gold and silver; your garments were fine linen, silk, and embroidered cloth. Fine flour, honey, and oil were your food. You were exceedingly beautiful, with the dignity of a queen. You were renowned among the nations for your beauty, perfect as it was, because of my splendor which I had bestowed on you, says the Lord God [Ezek. 16:3, 6–14].

But although the dialogue is begun by God, it never degenerates into a monologue, still less into an act of dictation. God lets people raise objections against him. In fact, knowledge of God is obtained by means of a struggle between God and Israel.

Jacob was left there alone. Then some man wrestled with him until the break of dawn. When the man saw that he could not prevail over him, he struck Jacob's hip at its socket, so that the hip socket was wrenched as they wrestled. The man then said, "Let me go, for it is daybreak." But Jacob said, "I will not let you go until you bless me." "What is your name?" the man said. He answered, "Jacob." Then the man said, "You shall no longer be spoken of as Jacob, but as Israel, because you have contended with divine and human beings and have prevailed" [Gen. 32:25–30].

The psalter is full of reproaches directed to God by people at prayer. "Lord, why?" "Lord, how long?" A superficial conception of biblical inspiration has allowed the reading of such constant reproaches in the Psalms to disillusion the overrationalistic mind: "How is it possible," they ask, "for the Holy Spirit to be the author of such words? Why, in some cases they are almost blasphemous, in others they betray an unloving kind of indignation!"

The paradox here is that though the reproaches are indeed extreme they bring light and peace to the anguished human heart. Dialogue with God must not be conducted in the artificial langauge of diplomacy, thus silencing the depths of anguish, anger, and despair that the presence of the divine mystery really breaks open in the human heart. In addressing God we must speak as we really are; we must tell God all our wretchedness, limitations, anguish, and lack of understanding. The biblical inspiration of the psalter guarantees the legitimacy of this kind of outspoken dialogue to which God is willing to subject himself when he initiates this unbroken conversation with humankind.

The balance characteristic of the Bible consists in uniting these two paradoxical extremes, making it possible to avoid the two causes why the dialogue is broken off and, with it, any genuine communication between people and God.

One cause is the immanentist conception of religion. In this view, religious truth must dwell exclusively in the sanctuary of the human conscience. Religion is a monologue the person carries on with himself, as he imagines a pseudoreality which is in fact only the product of his own subconsciousness and unconscious. The immanentist conception of religion is the legitimate child of all those pantheistic and idolatrous metaphysics that strip reality of its true created character.

Conversion to Christianity or Judaism requires a metaphysical conversion in which a person casts aside pantheistic metaphysics and accepts the metaphysics of the Bible. There is required what St. Paul called a "renewal of the mind." This metaphysical conversion involves, first of all, ceasing to idolize created reality—"They . . . say to a piece of wood, 'You are my father,' and to a stone, 'You gave me birth' " (Jer. 2:27)—and acknowledging that self-sufficiency, stability, and eternity are not attributes of the created order. This latter fact is clearly brought home to us by what we know of the world. The very existence of the world, given the world's radical insufficiency in the order of being, requires another, distinct from itself, in whom its stability can be grounded. "Whatever can be known about God is clear to them; he himself made it so. Since the creation of the world, invisible realities, God's eternal power and divinity, have become visible, recognized through the things he has made. Therefore these men are inexcusable" (Rom. 1:19–20).[2]

This implies that immanentism means a breaking off of dialogue not only between the person and God but also between the person and things, the person and the world. It means a proud and suicidal introversion.

The other reason why people break off the dialogue is because they misconceive and exaggerate the transcendence of God.

It is on the ground between these two extremes of immanence and misconceived transcendence that the dialogue of humankind with God, as shown in the Bible, is carried on. For our part we must have humility enough not to make of ourselves an exalted solitary in the realm of existence. We must accept all that falls within the scope of our perceptual powers, examine it and investigate it, even if we cannot exhaust its intelligibility. Before he accepts the mystery of God, the Christian must adopt the outlook of the Bible and accept the other, that which is distinct from himself; then, through this other, he can come into direct contact with the Other, his Creator, and speak to him.

It is precisely the evident transcendence of the Other— that is, God—that, far from simply causing a bottomless and impassable abyss between himself and humankind, bridges all distance in intimate dialogue. According to the Bible, God is not an unapproachable being but, on the contrary, is completely within reach. He can be approached by love, above all else. In fact, love is the first requisite for the dialogue: "You shall love the Lord, your God, with all your heart, and with all your soul, and with all your strength" (Deut. 6:5).

Perhaps the most interesting (and most scandalous) aspect of the relationship, however, is the fact that according to the biblical rules for dialogue with God we can bring reproaches against God! This means that acceptance of the divine mystery does not imply leaving off the intellectual search in which we attempt, humbly but boldly, to penetrate the dense thicket of the divine. On the contrary, the search for "knowledge," regarded as a free and responsible effort on our part, is required of us in the dialogue with God. Paul tells us that the pagans cannot be excused, because "they certainly had knowledge of God, yet they did not glorify him as God or give him thanks" (Rom 1:20–21); he implies here that if these people did not have this knowledge, they would not have been guilty.

The fact that God cannot be intellectually comprehended has provided many a lazy preacher with an invalid excuse for thinking himself freed of any obligation to make an intellectual effort to search out the mystery. Perhaps we can venture to say that the development of a "kerygmatic theology" has given a pretext for such an anti-intellectual and pseudopastoral attitude, even though this kind of (illegitimate) offspring was never intended or foreseen by the first-rate theologians who argued for a "kerygmatic theology."

"Kerygmatic theology" claimed to be a return to the method used by the Apostles for effectively presenting the Gospel message to nonbelievers. Dogmatic theology would have its place only once the message had been accepted. The message itself enters the mind in a prescientific way; that is why even today direct preaching aims at a prescientific kind of presentation. "Kerygma," in short, is the preaching of divine revelation as it sprang originally from the mouth of the Preacher sent by God. The "kerygmatic" looks directly to people, and ever since the Word became flesh salvation has been given only in the direct mutual encounter of kerygma and hearer (cf. Rom. 10:14).[3]

In the last analysis, despite their express disclaimers, the authors of this "kerygmatic" method are trying to strip the presentation of the message of all the "theological" ornamentation with which intellectual efforts have surrounded it. In so doing, they risk separating elements that were never separated even in apostolic times. We cannot find anywhere in the New Testament the purely "kerygmatic" formulations that the theologians of proclamation so eagerly seek. The kerygma is embedded in a theology, and the latter is not always as embryonic as has been thought. Even the synoptic writers preserve Jesus' preaching for us in literary forms that in turn presuppose earlier catechetical and homiletic forms; all these forms already represent a "theology," that is, a reflection on the original message.

There is no point, then, in trying to separate the "kerygmatic" from the "theological" or "dogmatic." It would be more honest simply to admit that theology has become so abstract and inflexible that it cannot effectively make its way into the minds of our contemporaries. The solution, therefore, is not to offer homage to a particular dogmatic theology and put it on a pedestal in a museum, while giving precedence in real life to a paradogmatic theology. The solution is to revise our particular theology, to rise above it, to go beyond it and elaborate new formulations (dogmatic ones) that will enable the message to penetrate the modern mentality.

As a result of this dangerous divorce between the theological and the kerygmatic, the attempt has even been made to proceed directly to evangelization without first engaging in apologetics. There is no doubt, of course, that apologetics has fallen upon sad times. This may be why we have lost all respect for it. On the other hand, the immense tomes of dogmatic theology cannot be given directly to a public that thinks in completely different categories. Yet we must admit that in talking with those in direct contact with the people, those who are working to win over today's pagans, we are in touch with people who have already learned to think in a new way.[4]

In short, the kerygmatic is not opposed to the dogmatic. Paul himself is a good example of how one officially assigned to proclaim the Christian event also reflects on its content, enriches it on the intellectual side, and presents it to his contemporaries. Paul would be unable to distinguish between his role as herald and his role as theologian. We should not, therefore, try to rend the living unity of the kerygmatic and the dogmatic. When the Church asks its theologians to reflect upon the Christian event, it always has in view the penetration of the message into the mind of the contemporary world.

The person who preaches in the Church's name should not be just an old hand who mouths a few rudiments of the Christian message in an archaic form. He should rather be a person of theological maturity, one who engages in an up-to-date, vital kind of theological reflection. One and the same person should, in this situation, be both herald (keryx) and theologian—a person who is, on the one hand, one "sent," dynamic, and moved by the Spirit, and, on the other, one of intellectual maturity. The vital synthesis of kerygma and dogma that we find in Paul is one that we must bear in mind and try to emulate.

In chapter 14 of the First Epistle to the Corinthians Paul emphasizes the necessity of reflecting and gaining a deeper knowledge of the Christian message. He gives first place among the charisms to the prophet, that is, the one who brings an intelligible message. Glossolalia may help the one praying but it is useless to the hearer, for he understands nothing of it. This is why there can be prophecy without speaking in tongues, but not the reverse (cf. 14:1–6). It is not enough for the charismatic to be exalted "in spirit," or in the affective or emotional part of himself; reflective awareness is also needed. The ideal of inspiration is that it should renew and enlarge the understanding, not suppress it (12–17). The Corinthians should develop their minds and intellectual grasp. The destruction of fleshly wisdom (ch. 1) should by no means degenerate into brutalization! If Christians are bidden to become as children, it is innocence, not ignorance, that is meant (14:20). In all this, Paul is emphasizing the "intellectual" character of his own theology and pastoral practice. The urgent task of adapting the message so that people can understand it requires an enormous intellectual effort.

Such, then, is dialogue between humankind and God, as the Bible teaches it. It is at once humble and bold. Humble, because it accepts the existence of the other and the Other, even if that existence is perceived and seen through the veil of mystery. Bold, because it dares to confront God and ask him to explain his behavior toward us.

The dialogue can be broken off in two ways: through the human pride that thinks itself the only true existent (solipsism) and through a "devout" laziness that fails to make the intellectual effort needed for a deeper knowledge of the mystery.

Once the dialogue is broken off, God disappears from our purview, and what Nietzsche calls the death of God then occurs. But such a deicide is due, in the last analysis, to our will: to the pride that gives rise to immanentism, or to the "saintly" laziness of the devout who claim to be enlightened and therefore culpably neglect to approach the mystery of transcendence on the intellectual level.

ATHEISM, A HIDDEN DANGER
FOR A SOCIETY PHARISAICALLY CHRISTIAN

The dialogue of God with humankind does not take place within the isolated individual. God speaks with *people,* and people as a community face God in a collective way. This means that dialogue spreads by contagion, as it were, and that an "apostle" cannot effectively speak of God to others unless they see him engaged in vital dialogue with God.

The origin of modern atheism within the bosom of Christianity itself lies in the breaking off of dialogue with God that is typical of many militant Christians, especially preachers and apologists. They speak of God as "he," as simply an object of the intellect. They do not come forward as Moses and Aaron did to the people of Israel after having spoken with God in the burning bush.

The result is that communication with God has been cut off. The ex-Christian, still nostalgic for his earlier state, tries desperately to get through to God, but, horrified and impatient, all he hears is a busy signal.

In a noteworthy philosophical essay Albert Camus has made a number of very interesting remarks on what he calls "metaphysical revolt," revolt against unqualified evil or evil in itself. He makes a noble but despairing effort to find some formula that will effectively channel the revolt, a revolt that can help in leading humankind to a less unjust condition, even if the total disappearance of injustice does not seem even remotely possible. To achieve his purpose, Camus thinks he must renounce transcendence, but he cannot deny the great nostalgia for it that becomes almost an obsession with him.

The protest against evil which is at the very core of metaphysical revolt is significant in this regard. It is not the suffering of a child, which is repugnant in itself, but the fact that the suffering is not justified. . . . The rebel obstinately confronts a world condemned to death and the impenetrable obscurity of the human condition with his demand for life and absolute clarity. He is seeking, without knowing it, a moral philosophy or a religion. Rebellion, even though it is blind, is a form of asceticism. Therefore, if the rebel blasphemes, it is in the hope of finding a new god. He staggers under the shock of the first and most profound of all religious experiences, but it is a disenchanted religious experience.[5]

That last phrase puts it exactly: "a disenchanted religious experience." The human being is relentlessly pursued by the transcendent. All the paths he follows in order to rise above himself inevitably steer him toward something infinite and holy.

In principle, the rebel only wanted to conquer his own existence and to maintain it in the face of God. But he forgets his origins and, by the law of spiritual imperialism, he sets out in search of world conquest by way of an infinitely multiplied series of murders.[6]

We Christians know that our task is to lead others to transcendence. Not only do we have a wonderful message of redemption and all-embracing salvation; we are also able to show the world this redemption and salvation being effectively brought to fruition before the eyes of all. The "good news" is not just a verbal message. It is a breakthrough of divine power into the sphere of the Church, which is open to all comers.

Confronted as we are by the blasphemous attitude of the anguished rebel who, without realizing it, is waiting for a new god, we must slough off our own pharisaical attitude of sanctimonious primness. In its stead we must develop the deeply Christian outlook that bears vital witness and thus shows others the path to transcendence. Ours must be a dialogue with God the echoes of which will be perceptible to the human community in which we live.

Now that a century stands between us and him, the German philosopher Friedrich Nietzsche seems clad in the long, torn robes of an old, itinerant biblical prophet. After his anguished cry that "God is dead," he looks out on a Western world which, though wholly shaped by Christianity, can no longer rely on that Christianity, for that world has discovered, to its surprise and horror, that behind the facade of Christianity lies only emptiness and nothingness. Nietzsche writes:

Christianity has created a fake world whose non-truth we finally recognize thanks to the instinct for truth that Christianity itself has fostered. There is now nothing left of that world, for in Christianity everything coherent and valuable was but pretense. As soon as this fact is acknowledged, life crumbles in a way men have never experienced before. The time has come when we must pay for having been Christians for two thousand years. No longer do we carry the heavy weight that forces us to go on living; for a while we do not know what to do. At present everything is totally false.

For a century we have gone on contrasting Nietzsche's "prophetic" lamentation with the varied experiences people really have. But meanwhile the camouflaged atheism of many Christian groups that still influenced the history of the Western world during that century was producing a vacuum around the "Christian civilization" they extolled. For, in fact, at the heart of that civilization there was a fearful absence of authentic evangelical values.

Fortunately, the better Catholic writers, theologians included, are today uttering a heartfelt *Confiteor* in face of the undeniable fact that the West has, from a Christian viewpoint, become degenerate.

A new historical movement has sprung up in the name of the values that Christianity should have preserved but has in fact betrayed: in the name of justice, of the poor, of the worker. This movement has made its own the eminently biblical and evangelical demand for the liberation of the oppressed and turned against those who should have championed the oppressed but have in fact been, actively or passively, on the side of the oppressor. God is calling us back, by means of Marxism, to a truth and a demand we should never have forgotten. In St. Paul's expression, we have made truth the prisoner of injustice. Until we recover possession of the truth that Marxism brings us, persecution will not cease.[7]

According to the old biblical view, to which Augustine gave a generalized form in his *City of God,* God permits the great social evils in order through them to direct the course of history. From this point of view, we must ask which of the two worlds that now confront each other will be better prepared to undertake the anxious search for God that lies ahead for a wearied and surfeited humankind. Will it be the Marxist world with its strong sense of life as a struggle and forward movement? Or the Western world which has developed the technology to satisfy its immediate desires?

The Marxist has spent many years dreaming of a better world of class equality, utopian peace, and universal coexistence among the world's inhabitants. But as soon as his zeal in the struggle for immediate betterment grows cool and he too, like the Westerner, achieves the technology for satisfying his temporal aspirations, he becomes aware of the vacuum left by the cessation of biological struggle.

The Westerner, not so. He never feels the sheer biological energy of creation through struggle. He will end in the rosy nihilism that we see, for example, in the novels of Françoise Sagan.

Preachers of a renewed Gospel will find more ready hearers in areas influenced by Marxism than in the decadent groups that make up our Western world, filled as it is with its refrigerators and coldly satisfied with its own incredible superficiality.

THE LIVING GOD OF ABRAHAM, ISAAC, AND JACOB

Martin Buber relates that at a school for adults in a city of Central Germany he once spoke for three successive evenings on "Religion as Reality."[8] The speaker's only purpose was to explain that " 'faith' is not a feeling in the soul of man but an entrance into reality." The proposition is simple enough, but it is not the way we usually think of faith; this is why Buber felt he needed three evenings to get it across, and even then he needed not only the three talks but the three discussions that followed them.

During the discussions he noted the disheartening fact that though the audience consisted largely of workers, none of them said anything. It was the students, and some others, that expressed questions, objections, and doubts; the workers said nothing. At the end of the third session he found out why this was, when "a young worker came up to me and said: 'Do you know, we can't speak in there, but if you would meet with us tomorrow, we could talk together the whole time.' Of course I agreed."

The next day, a Sunday, they gathered after dinner and conversed all evening. One of the workers, not a young man, attracted the speaker's attention, because he was listening like someone who really wanted to hear; he was a man with an unusual face. Finally he spoke up, using words supposedly spoken by Laplace in conversation with Napoleon: "I have had the experience that I do not need this hypothesis 'God' in order to be quite at home in the world." He pronounced "hypothesis" as though he had heard it from a famous scientist who had taught in that school and recently died at the age of eighty-five. The latter did not object to having his idea of nature called "God," but he used the same tone of voice and the same language whether he was dealing with zoology or with his conception of the world.

The philosopher tried to grasp the man's viewpoint and attempted to show him that the subjective world of the senses and sensation is mysteriously connected with a world of "other" realities, both worlds, however, being problematic. Therefore certain questions necessarily arose.

How could we in our thinking place together these worlds so divorced from one another? What was the being that gave this "world," which had become so questionable, its foundation?

When I was through a stern silence ruled in the now twilit room. Then the man . . . raised his heavy lids, which had been lowered the whole time, and said slowly and impressively, "You are right."

I sat in front of him dismayed. What had I done: I had led the man to the threshold beyond which there sat enthroned the majestic image which the great physicist, the great man of faith, Pascal, called the God of the Philosophers. Had I wished for that? Had I not rather wished to lead him to the Other, Him whom Pascal called the God of Abraham, Isaac, and Jacob, Him to whom one can say Thou?

It grew dusk, it was late. On the next day I had to depart. I could not remain, as I now ought to do; I could not enter into the factory where the man worked, become his comrade, live with him, win his trust through real life relationship, help him to walk with me the way of the creature who *accepts* the creation. I could only return his gaze.

One night in 1654, after several hours of ecstatic trance, Pascal wrote a few hurried lines. Under the heading "Fire," we read his prayer: "God of Abraham, God of Isaac, God of Jacob, not of the philosophers and scholars."

Pascal was not trying to assert the irrationality of the idea of God or the conceptual improbability of his existence, but simply to state the inadequacy of philosophy alone to reach God. For this French physicist the form of concupiscence to which philosophers were especially tempted was pride; they offer their neighbor not God but their own systems.

"OUR DAILY GOD"

The great purpose of human avarice is to hoard. We want every-thing under our control so that we will not have to take thought for future eventualities.

Yet the human being is the only animal to whom life is not given ready made, so that by his own free efforts he may determine its shape. He is not an animal of the kind that grows in a determined fashion according to completely unalterable laws. No: he shapes himself by his own decisions, and he must continuously make these decisions. He does not have the luxury of making a once-and-for-all decision that would dispense him from the effort of making continuous small decisions. This state of affairs is due to the freedom which is humankind's great privilege and great re-sponsibility as well.

Now, the only effective way of shaping one's life is to answer God's call. God invites us to form ourselves according to a definite plan; if we follow it, we are guaranteed the conquest of our alienations.

Thus viewed, religion is simply a humanism or, better, *the* proper humanism; it is the only effective way of reaching the goal of which the human person dreamed ever since he began to drag himself painfully across the face of our world.

We encounter God, and the encounter makes some decision necessary. The decision, freely taken, will set our life in motion in a definite direction. If our decision is to believe, then we acknowl-edge our powerlessness to make ourselves what we should be and we abandon ourselves into the hands of the living God so that with his help we may shape our own lives with hope and with the assurance that some day we will reach human fulfillment.

But we would badly deceive ourselves if we thought that this acceptance of God is only a solemn act that takes place once and for all when we make our religious choice. As long as we remain in this state of pilgrimage, we must go on shaping our lives, and that means we must be continually making decisions.

We must choose God each day as we did on the day of our baptism when our religious life began. That is why prayer, which is the action in which we decide and choose God, must be repeated daily and indeed almost hourly. We must pray without ceasing to "our daily God."

NOTES

1. Waldo Frank, *The Rediscovery of Man: A Memoir and a Methodology of Modern Life* (New York: Braziller, 1958), p. 330.

2. Tresmontant, *Estudios,* p. 117.

3. Cf. Hugo Rahner, *A Theology of Proclamation,* trans. Richard Dimler et al. (New York: Herder and Herder, 1968); Josef A. Jungmann, *Handing on the Faith: A Manual of Catechetics* (New York: Herder and Herder, 1959); J.R. Geiselmann, *Jesus der Christus,* rev. ed. (Munich: Kösel, 1956); J.A. Ubieta, "El kerygma apostólico y los evangelios," *Estudios Biblicos* 18 (1959): 21–26; D. Grasso, S.J., "Il kerygma e la predicazione," *Gregorianum* 41 (1960): 424–50.

4. Jacques Loew, *Journal d'une mission ouvrière* (Paris: Cerf, 1959), pp. 143–84.

5. Albert Camus, *The Rebel: An Essay on Man in Revolt,* trans. Anthony Bower (New York: Knopf, 1961), p. 101.

6. Ibid., p. 103.

7. Tresmontant, *Estudios,* pp. 153–55.

8. Martin Buber, *Eclipse of God: Studies in the Relation between Religion and Philosophy* (New York: Harper & Row, 1952). Buber's account, here reproduced almost verbatim, and the quotations from it are from pp. 3–6.

CHAPTER 4

CHRISTIAN FAITH: EXISTENTIAL ATTITUDE OF SELF-FORMATION

The human person is a being who is in process of being formed, and it is he himself who does the forming. The whole problem he faces can be reduced to the quest for existential fulfillment and for the most effective way of achieving that fulfillment. In modern times Marxism has laid heavy stress on the idea that a philosophy must not be content with merely interpreting life in a theoretical way, but must also effectively change it and direct its course.

The great human question, therefore, has been and continues to be this: How is the human person to form himself?

St. Paul, especially in his Epistle to the Galatians, describes two opposed existential attitudes, each claiming to answer the great question; these attitudes he calls *kauchesis,* or ''boasting,'' and ''faith.''

KAUCHESIS

Kauchesis was the attitude Paul found in many Jews, especially in the Pharisees. They acknowledged God and accepted his law, but they claimed to be able to attain the human ideal set forth by the law by their own native powers. They rejected grace or at least did not consider it necessary. The result was devastating, since by our own power we cannot overcome the great alienating forces of sin and death (cf. Gal. 2:16–21; 3:10–14; 4:21–31; 5:1–12).

Rabbinic theology had gradually become infected by a genuine "worship of the law." The law had developed into an autonomous entity, the possession of which was a guarantee of all blessings. The Torah, foremost of all creatures, was the first thing created by God, and it was indeed created, that is, it existed as an extramental reality and not simply in the mind. It lived at God's side, among his treasures, as his daughter, his beloved. This kind of preexistence, asserted in various sources, makes of the law a supernatural being; Pseudo-Aristeas and Philo call it divine.[1]

It is quite understandable that once the law has been thus divinized it should be considered to exercise a real causality in making people "just." The power to do so is inherent in the law; we need only take possession of the law through attentive study and meditation; once the law is installed in the mind of the instructed scholar it communicates all kinds of blessings to him.

Summing up this "legalistic" attitude, which is represented above all by Pharisaism, Bonsirven thus describes its roots:

What are the defects [of a Pharisaic morality]? There are deficiencies that come from an exaggeration of human dignity: Man as king of creation tends to become the center of creation as well; his liberty, not lessened by any original sin, is adequate for overcoming all his evil inclinations; and he does not feel the need of any positive divine help. Here is an attitude analogous to Stoicism, and one that anticipates the Pelagian heresies.

Deficiencies arising from legalism are more serious, and these make themselves felt to the extent that Pharisaism wins predominance and imposes its views. The Torah is reverenced as the sovereign authority to which even God submits. . . . The study of the law is presented as the great commandment; in theory, knowledge is superior to right action; holiness and piety cannot be attained by the unlettered, who deserve only scorn and condemnation; only the scholar can be a saint. . . .

Nonetheless we do not think that these deviations meant the total disappearance of the great principles of Jewish morality and its high ideal of justice and charity. But they did give rise in many souls to feelings of self-sufficiency and to a formalist outlook that is the sister of hypocrisy—attitudes not to be found in the prophets or the psalmists.[2]

Bonsirven wrote these lines in 1935. The validity of his final judgment has since been confirmed by the discovery of the Qumran documents, for these show how beneath the surface that was formed by official Pharisaism the spiritual stream that rises in the prophets and psalmists continues to run ever fresh and unchanged.

The spiritual life of the Community [of the "sons of Zadok"] was wholly based on personal vocation; each member had been called and set aside by God. They were, every one of them, the "children of grace."

However eminent the part they assigned to the study and the practice of the Law they were nonetheless convinced that wisdom, justice and sanctity were the fruits of grace. . . .

Through considering God's mercies towards them, the brethren were brought to the knowledge of their own nothingness, and abased themselves before the infinite greatness of God. Such an attitude is dramatically opposed to what is (inaccurately) described as "Pharisaic" piety. . . .

A brother, so far from boasting of his scrupulous observance of the Law, was ever tormented by the recollection of his past faults, and felt unworthy of the mercies shown to him by God. He was well aware of his weakness and evil inclinations, and was urged thereby to surrender his whole self to God completely. In his relations with God, humility and trust were his most outstanding characteristics.[3]

The antithesis Paul sees between "boasting" (Jewish or pagan) and faith is based less on the intellectual content of each than on the contrasting attitudes they adopt to God who reveals himself. "Boasting" describes a purely intellectual, logical attitude, and implies the claim to advance solely by its own powers.

It is only against this understanding of what Paul means by "boasting" that we can grasp his presentation of faith as a dynamic, existential human attitude. "In Christ Jesus neither circumcision nor the lack of it counts for anything; only faith, which expresses itself through love" (Gal. 5:6).

"In Christ Jesus": that is, when a person is aroused to love by the great event of the dynamic presence of Christ who brings salvation. In the face of this saving event, "Neither circumcision nor the lack of it counts for anything"; neither one has any value as an effective means of salvation or in the efficacious quest of that human fulfillment toward which we cannot but tend. Paul puts on one and the same level, as far as impotence with regard to salvation is concerned, the proud attitude of the Jew who is content simply to possess his law and the equally self-sufficient attitude of the pagan who thinks that knowledge is enough to lead him to fulfillment (cf. Rom. 1:16–21).

Both attitudes are at bottom identical, for both are *purely intellectual*. They acknowledge that the object of knowledge must be sought outside themselves; they acknowledge God as the source of the material for thought, either through revelation of the law (the Jews) or through the revelation whose instrument is *logos* or reason (the pagans). In his Epistle to the Galatians, however, Paul brings out the helplessness of the Jew in face of the program drawn up for him in the law; the mere rational possession and intellectual acceptance of the law are not enough to enable us to put it into practice. Then, in chapter 7 of the Epistle to the Romans, Paul describes in a masterful way the helplessness of the pagan (that is, humankind generally) to do what he knows and acknowledges intellectually to be the right thing. The "Gnostic" may even "desire" what is good, but he will not succeed in putting it into practice by his own unaided strength (cf. Rom. 7:18).

Faith, on the contrary, acknowledges God not only as the logical truth but as the ontological truth as well and as the only source of a vital power that can enable us to overcome our own radical impotence. Now we can understand Paul when he contrasts the powerlessness of "boasting" (circumcision or noncircumcision) with the full power of faith for salvation. Faith, we now see, is not a mere intellectual attitude, but an energy and a dynamism which, expressing itself "through love," puts us on the way to salvation and fulfillment.

Throughout his exposition of the contrasts Paul is not talking of whether a given person is saved or not saved; he is talking of the *ability* to reach salvation. He always speaks of the person as such, moving along a road as did Abraham, the great pilgrim; his only concern is to inquire whether a given path leads to the goal or leads away from it. "Boasting" acknowledges the markers set along the way, but it trusts, vainly, in the strength of its own feet. Its trust leads it nowhere.

The experience of Israel, which St. Paul describes for us so vividly and profoundly, has been renewed throughout Christian history. Heresies of the Pelagian type reduced faith to a purely intellectual adherence to a highly rationalized creed and to the acceptance of a fine moral code; for a person to be able to live by the code he need only belong to the Christian clan. Thus the luminous darkness of the mystery which the Church preaches was reduced to the simple clarity of "Christendom."

"Boasting" gradually permeated extensive areas of the various "christendoms." Faith was replaced by a system neatly set forth in catechetical propositions, and was turned thus into an official endorsement of social situations which existed for the comfort and ease of a few leaders or heads. Many Christians succumbed to the temptation of the disciples on Mount Tabor, and instead of the risks involved in being wrapped about by the luminous cloud of faith and the divine word they preferred the security of their miserable tents and ugly encampments. But in the face of this proud decision by people who should be Christians the cloud withdrew, and on the summit of Tabor there reigned the ominous silence of God.

Martin Buber was right when he reproached Sartre for having taken God's silence as his starting point without also asking how much of the silence was due to our not hearing or not having heard.[4]

To sum up: St. Paul shows us the problem involved in "boasting," a problem that is not lessened simply because the individual accepts the "logical" superiority of God, that is, pays tribute to God as an idea. For, as we have seen, we cannot by our own powers carry out God's plan for us, and therefore we must inevitably fall into extreme and unqualified despair. In such a mental impasse, pride will urge us to deny the existence of this troublesome being who requires us to reach an impossible goal. As a matter of historical fact, the attitudes that arise out of "boasting"—Pelagianism, pharisaic ritualism, excessive involvement with riches and power, etc.—have inevitably led to militant atheism.

"Contrary to the opinion of certain of his Christian critics, Nietzsche did not form a project to kill God. He found Him dead in the soul of his contemporaries."[5]

FAITH

Throughout the Old Testament faith has some special characteristics that prevent it from being quite what we moderns think of as faith (a purely intellectual adherence to a truth proposed to us from without).

The word *pistis* in the Greek Bible usually translates a word based on the Hebrew root *aman* and thus expresses the divine property of steadiness, solidity, or consistency, by reason of which God can be called a rock or stone, a fortress, etc., as contrasted with all that is fragile, weak, and inconstant.

To a Greek, truth meant the "uncovering of what had been hidden" (*a-letheia*). To a Roman, whose outlook was formed by juridical principles, truth was authenticity, that is, "that which is confirmed by documents." To a Hebrew, truth was "that which is sure and solid" (*emet*). The Greek verb *pisteuein* (to believe) translates the causative form of a Hebrew verb which means, literally, "to become firm, solid," by sharing in the firmness and solidity of God.

Yahweh is a reliable God (*né'èman*) whom one can trust unreservedly (Deut. 7:9), and the odd-sounding personification of Christ as the "Amen" (Rev. 3,4) carries the same overtones. The word *Amen* expresses the solidity proper to a commitment within the framework of the covenant. Mount Gerazim and Mount Ebal heard the repercussions of that commitment (Deut. 27:12–26); Nehemiah required it of the repentant Zionists (Neh. 5:13). To believe (*hé'èmin*) means precisely to rely on Him who deserves, by his very nature, an unlimited trust; man trusts in God without qualification because God is what he is (Gen. 15:6). Faith is this attitude of total trust.[6]

When Israel stops *believing,* that is, *relying on* God, and tries to live on its own wretched resources, it inevitably falls into insecurity, anxiety, and despair. "Among these nations you will find no repose, not a foot of ground to stand upon, for there the Lord will give you an anguished heart and wasted eyes and a dismayed spirit. You will live in contant suspense and stand in dread both day and night, never sure of your existence" (Deut. 28:65–66).

Israel will never be "sure of its existence," that is, it will not find within its own being a basis for solidity and security. We find the same expression in Job 24:22–23, where God is said to intervene in behalf of him "who rises without assurance of his life," that is, who abandons the support and security he had thought to find in himself, for it was in reality a false security.

The idea of faith as the existential attitude of "being in" finds energetic expression in Paul's words: "The life I live now is not my own; Christ is living in me" (Gal. 2:20).

The literary use of "I," which St. Paul begins in the lines just quoted, continues and expands in Romans 7, which opens up for us the true meaning of the words in Galatians. In this chapter of Romans the Apostle gives us a clear and concrete definition of the "I": "I am weak flesh sold into the slavery of sin" (Rom. 7:14). Throughout the chapter he sketches with broad strokes the biography of the "I." "I" did not know sin until the law came; when the law came, sin, which had been lurking in the depths of the "I," hurled itself upon the "I" and inflicted a deadly wound. Since that point, the "I" has dragged out a wretched existence, unable to attain the vital ideal that was still present in the mind. The "I" was really in a wretched state, says Paul, and who could free it from the impoverished existence that it faced until death? "Only the grace of Jesus Christ!" says the Saint in exultant tones.

As we can see, the "I" is the historical person in his real, concrete existence, as seen by the Old Testament; it is a vision that Paul develops and completes, especially in the Epistle to the Romans. "I" is the person in his proud isolation, separated from God and thrown back on his own pitiful resources. "I" cannot in any sense really live, for the "I" is doomed to failure and death.

All this explains why Paul can say that once he had died to the law together with Christ, the "I" no longer lived—i.e., the sinful, tragic human person—but Christ lived in its place. He is not describing an individual experience, some mystical summit that he would have reached in a series of transformations; he is describing the condition proper to every Christian. There has indeed been a radical change: The "I"—the person as such, who is doomed to sin and death—has been changed into the person-in-Christ, reconciled with God and able now to conquer death for good.

Christ is the source of life. What life is meant? For Paul, as for any Semite, life is a highly concentrated, univocal concept. Life is our concrete existence; everything that lessens our happiness and brings us nearer to that end which is death is the opposite of life. Now, this full life, which is identical with happiness, can only be conceived and characterized in the presence of God. A genuine possibility of living is possible only in view of the central fact of Christ's resurrection: If Christ had not engaged in a definitive struggle with death, we could not believe that he had redeemed us from sin, for sin and death had been, historically, united in a causal interdependence.

For this reason the concept of life in Paul always has an essential relation to resurrection. Neither Paul nor any other New Testament writer ever uses "life" in a purely "spiritual" sense, as meaning a moral attitude toward God or even as a sharing in the divine being.

For this reason, too, the Christian's life before his resurrection is, in Paul's eyes, only a hope of life (cf. Rom. 6:8; 8:11, 17, 23, 24; 1 Cor. 15:20, 22, 26), or, if it is called "life," this is only because it is the first fruits (1 Cor. 15:20; Rom. 8:23) or pledge or assurance of the resurrection (Eph. 1:14; 2 Cor. 1:22).

The continual survival of the "I"—of the historical, sinful, mortal person—is nullified by the light of faith and hope: "I still live my human life, but it is a life of faith in the Son of God, who loved me and gave himself for me" (Gal. 2:20). Paul is referring here to the tension between present and future that is characteristic of the intermediate state of "reconciliation" when we are freed from sin but not yet fully saved through the resurrection (cf. Rom. 5:10).

We thus continue to live "in the flesh," which means that we continue to lead an ephemeral existence upon which sin has left its mark. But at the center of this impoverished existence a lamp has been lit: faith in the Son of God. This faith assures us that we can overcome the "flesh" and pass over in an irreversible way to the "spirit," that is, to the full existence that follows upon resurrection. We believe that this is possible because of the great event of Christ's redemptive death; he "loved me and gave himself for me." The "I" has been rescued by the love of Christ who, by his death, has released it from this present pitiful, ephemeral existence and put it on the path to a "full" eternal life in the presence of God.

Now Paul expresses the humble, grateful attitude of the "I" as it realizes God's great gift: "I will not treat God's gracious gift as pointless. If justice is available through the law, then Christ died to no purpose!" (Gal. 2:21). The "I" is no longer proud and self-sufficient; it realizes that God's free "gift" ("grace") alone can bestow justification and the possibility of finally conquering death, or, in short, of reaching existential fulfillment.

FAITH IS A DIVINE INITIATIVE

In Gal. 3:6–9, Paul introduces for the first time the magnificent figure of Abraham, and around it begins to weave the Christian midrash that will contain his whole understanding of salvation.

Rabbinic exegesis had played down the importance of Abraham's faith, for it measured that faith by the petty norms of the impoverished casuistry that had been developed in the rabbinic schools. We have a classic example of this minimization in the Book of Jubilees.[7] Almost directly upon mentioning the birth of Abraham the writer presents him as already a "religious man" whose exemplary conduct is in sharp contrast to the corrupt familial and national environment in which he lives.

And the child began to understand the errors of the earth that all went astray after graven images and after uncleanness, and his father taught him writing, and he was two weeks of years old, and he separated himself from his father, that he might not worship idols with him. And he began to pray to the Creator of all things that He might save him from the errors of the children of men.[8]

At this point in the narrative the writer brings in various wonderful things done by Abraham at an early age that show that the child was protected by God (11:18–24; 12:12). In 12:19 Abraham is shown uttering a prayer in which it seems that he chooses God, not that God chooses him! "My God, God Most High, Thou alone art my God, and Thee and Thy dominion have I chosen."[9]

Paul was undoubtedly familiar with this twisted interpretation of the story of Abraham and reacted strongly against it, especially in Romans 4. The story of Abraham, which begins in Genesis 12, has its starting point in a divine initiative: God promises Abraham an inheritance, or, as Paul puts it, he promises "Abraham and his descendents that they would inherit the world" (Rom. 4:13). Paul emphasizes this idea of inheritance, for it is well suited to bring out both the unmerited generosity of the giver and the lack of any activity on the part of the beneficiary.[10]

If Abraham had thought of presenting God with a record of good works so that he might win the promise, his action would have been useless, for his very history as a "religious man" begins with God's call. Abraham had lived the first seventy-five years of his life (cf. Gen. 12:4) in "godlessness," and in the eyes of the true God he was a man without any treasury of merits (cf. Rom. 4:4).

In brief, Abraham was "justified" by God and became a friend and authentic servant of God not because he had lived a life filled with *religious good works,* but because he believed and surrendered himself unconditionally to a God who made certain promises to him and took the step that was the start of Abraham's religious life. Abraham passed, in a single leap, from a life as a pagan and idolater to a life as a genuinely religious man, and the leap took the form of his act of faith. Circumcision, which in Jewish eyes was the great religious work, came much later, and its role was simply to be a "seal" upon that justification by faith that Abraham had acquired while still uncircumcised (Rom. 4:11).

Abraham, as his life is authentically interpreted by Paul, typifies faith as the existential attitude proper to "religious man." Faith is a sharing in the solidity of the only absolute being, God. God initiates the encounter and offers the support of his friendly arm. Faith, according to Paul, is always a gift of God.

FAITH BRINGS A RESULTANT HUMAN ACTIVITY

Faith is an existential attitude that begins with the acknowledgement of our own inability to overcome sin and death and turns trustingly to God, the Absolute, who promises his aid. The attitude is not a purely passive one, not just a "letting oneself go." It is essentially also a going or "journeying": from "Ur of the Chaldees," that is, from the nothingness of sin and death to "a land which God will show us," that is, justification and life. "Boasting" is different, for, while it too tries to reach God, it tries to do so with its own resources, claiming that we are able to make the journey on our own, without divine help.

In the great workshops of medieval theology the theologians were bent on an analysis of faith insofar as faith involves an intellectual affirmation. The viewpoint was a legitimate one and even necessary in practice, since a researcher must break down the object he is investigating and analyze its component parts. Unfortunately, when the controversy between Protestants and Catholics on justification broke out in the sixteenth century, both sides started with the partial concept of faith as intellectual affirmation and acted as if it were the whole.

The many Pauline texts that speak of faith as the *only* way to justification caused theologians to be divided into two irreconcilable camps. The Protestants claimed that, given a simple intellectual adherence to the word of God, justification automatically took place. The Catholic teaching authority categorically condemned that view and claimed that justification requires a "faith that expresses itself through love."[11]

But in authentic Pauline theology this problem does not even arise. The antithesis between faith and works does not refer to intellectual adherence and moral activity, or dogma and ethics. It refers rather to two attitudes that are both basically ethical attitudes: the attitude of self-sufficiency in which a person claims that he can make his way to God without God's help, and the attitude of humble faith in which a person acknowledges his own helplessness and takes the friendly arm of God who enables him to travel the road to fulfillment.

Given this meaning of the terms, Paul's direct and simple statement follows inexorably: Faith alone saves, works do not. That is: "works," or the proud purpose of the "boaster," do not bring a person to salvation; the only effective means is faith, the humble effort of the person who allows God's power to strengthen him.

Paul maintains that "love" explains the whole life of the person of faith. He is referring to that love of neighbor that is a "fruit of the Spirit" (Gal. 5:22). In chapter 13 of the First Epistle to the Corinthians he explains the whole of Christian morality as the detailed working out of fraternal love.

A few miles from Hebron, an ancient Palestinian city, lie the ruins of Mamre, where Abraham pitched his tents. There is a hill there which the Arabs still call Ramet-el-Jalil, or "hill of the friend." This is because to Muslims, as to Jews and Christians, Abraham was the friend of God.

Abraham represents the breakthrough into what we call the history of salvation. God has decided to approach us and to offer us the possibility of rising out of our tragic state. The first condition God requires is that he himself have the unquestioned initiative. Thus it is he who calls Abraham: "The Lord said to Abram: 'Go forth from the land of your kinsfolk and from your father's house to a land that I will show you' " (Gen. 12:1).

God's call is a demanding one, for, in order to respond, Abraham must leave his own country and his family and set out for an unknown country. But his acceptance, his immense act of faith, is not a purely passive gesture that will turn the patriarch into a puppet in God's hands. On the contrary, God looks for and requires his collaboration. The task he entrusts to Abraham is difficult; it will take decisiveness and perseverance to carry it out.

Moreover, God, master of the whole undertaking to save humankind, acquaints the great patriarch with his hidden plans and decisions. Thus one evening, God, along with two angels, appears to Abraham. The patriarch offers them hospitality in his tent, in accordance with the complicated rules of politeness current in the East. As they prepare to leave, Abraham thinks it his duty to accompany them part of the way; he does so and they come within sight of Sodom, the city of sin. Then "the Lord reflected: 'Shall I hide from Abraham what I am about to do, now that he is to become a great and populous nation, and all the nations of the earth are to find blessing in him?' " (Gen. 18:17–18). The Lord acknowledges that he cannot hide his plans from his friend Abraham, and enters upon an unrestricted dialogue with him. Abraham contends with the Lord in a desperate attempt to ward off the divine punishment that threatens the sinful city.

Ever since that time, the believer, the genuine believer, is always a friend of God. He accepts the divine plan without reservation, but then in deep humility dares to enter into dialogue with God, to let his feelings burst forth in God's presence, with simplicity to ask God for explanations, and to offer God his own ideas and his efforts.

The most mysterious thing about faith may well be not the unreserved acceptance of the divine call but the immense respect God has for the liberty of his friend the believer.

THE BELIEVER'S ACTION IS A SERIOUS ATTEMPT TO ACHIEVE OBJECTIVE EFFECTIVENESS

To God's action corresponds a genuine "reaction" in the believer. But the believer's action is not simply an occasion for proving his willingness, his "good intention"; it represents an explicit effort to do what is objectively the most effective thing, since what is at stake is the shaping of history and this must be done by means suitable for the purpose.

Throughout the Epistle to the Galatians we are given an insight into the uprightness of Paul's conscience. He is not forced to regret having omitted anything that would implement his pastoral zeal for the Galatian community. Yet Paul is not satisfied simply to have had a "good intention" while closing his eyes to the objective results of his toil. On the contrary, he is very anxious about these objective results: "I fear for you; all my efforts with you may have been wasted" (Gal. 4:11).

Paul often describes his apostolic ministry as "work" or "hard work" or "labor" (Greek *kopos, kopiazo*; cf. 2 Cor. 6:5; 10:15; 11:23, 27; Gal. 6:17; 1 Thess. 2:9; 3:5; 2 Thess. 3:8). But he does not think it enough simply to have done this apostolic "work" and to have no interest in its outcome; on the contrary, he suffers constantly from the fear of being ineffective. That is why he had gone up to Jerusalem: "to make sure the course I was pursuing, or had pursued, was not useless" (Gal. 2:2). He regarded the Philippians, a community of mature Christians, as a reason for legitimate pride on his part: "As I look to the day of Christ, you give me cause to boast that I did not run the race in vain or work to no purpose" (Phil. 2:16).

This desire to be able to present at the Judgment—on the "Day of the Lord"—solid apostolic achievements and not just "good intentions" is an old preoccupation of the Apostle.

If different ones build on this foundation with gold, silver, precious stones, wood, hay, or straw, the work of each one will be made clear. The Day [of the Lord, that is, the day of judgment] will disclose it. That day will make its appearance with fire, and fire will test the quality of each man's work. If the building a man has raised on this foundation still stands, he will receive his recompense; if a man's building burns, he will suffer loss. He himself will be saved, but only as one fleeing through fire [1 Cor. 3:12–15].

Whatever be the interpretation of the details of this passage, one point in it is clear: The good intentions of the worker are not enough; he must endeavor to do work that is objectively solid and permanent. The world, in Paul's eyes, is not a great sports arena where the divine referee appraises and rewards the skill of the players. It is a great construction site where people have received from the divine architect the commission to build according to definite plans and to produce a building that will last. "We are God's co-workers, while you are his cultivation, his building" (1 Cor. 3:9).

The anxious desire that his apostolic work be objectively effective led to great discouragement at times: "We were crushed beyond our strength, even to the point of despairing of life" (2 Cor. 1:8). Paul was a pioneer, a man who felt oppressed within the narrow walls of ancient religious structures that had become walking corpses. But the role of the pioneer is one of the most difficult, even if also one of the most fruitful, a person can have. It is the position of one who lives in his own times but clearly foresees that the walls of the rickety shed that history has built must soon come tumbling down. He lives within a social structure that has become an obstacle in the way of history.

Many others live in blissful unconcern, thinking that the structure will last forever, that it will survive simply because it has lasted this long. But the eyes of the pioneer are filled with the light of that future that is in a sense already present. He has the urge to reform. He wants to go through the streets and squares uttering the bitter, cutting cry of the prophet. But the people who live out their ant-like lives in the housing developments and on the subways and in the supermarkets drown out his voice with the anonymous noise of their streets. They go on with their closed-in little lives.

The pioneer grows weary and sits discouraged at the doors of others; despair sweeps over him and he falls into the pit of anguish. He is imprisoned with people who would live wholly in the past, and he cannot breathe the deadly air. To his dry lips rises the bitter question of discouragement: Why should I go on working?

Yet a searching analysis of the causes that influence the course of history will show the immense force exerted by the strenuous solitary efforts of the prophets and pioneers. Their work is the sapper's work: They mine the soil of history with a powerful charge, the effect of which is delayed, but immensely effective when it comes. They go through life hungry and in rags, loaded down with splendid ideas but wretchedly protected against the cold by a few greasy newspapers. But the ideas are irresistibly swept into the stream of history; there they draw strength from the waters and finally produce the lush growth that will beautify the riverbanks of life in the future.

It would be a mistake to try to avoid the suffering by slipping away from the present structure that must inevitably collapse and that we find so hard to endure. For it is only from within this structure that we can effectively work to change the structures history erects. It is thanks to the perseverance of the great solitary pioneers that history pursues its weary quest for fulfillment.

THE BELIEVER ON HIS JOURNEY

Our reflections on faith as an existential attitude cannot, of course, exhaust the rich treasures contained in the sources of our Christian theology. Nonetheless, it may be worthwhile to rest content with the light we already have and to try to see what it tells us of the believer's ordinary daily life.

The believer is not a person who runs away from the world around him to which he naturally belongs. On the contrary, his faith roots him ever more deeply in a world for whose progress he is responsible.

From the vantage point provided by faith, then, let us observe the course of daily life and reflect upon the necessary consequences of the attitude we have adopted in the effort to give meaning to our life as a whole.

A LEAP INTO THE VOID

As we have already said, faith is not a cold intellectual adherence to a list of abstract truths set before us by an external agency, even if that agency be called God. Faith is something far more profound: an existential attitude of the human person in the face of the divine call.

We live immersed in our own nothingness, our helplessness, our ontological weakness. We can adopt one of two attitudes to our situation. One is the attitude of pride or what St. Paul calls "boasting": the attitude of self-sufficiency, the belief that we can with our own wretched resources shape our lives and give an effective answer to the many questions which throng the mind and cause it so much anxiety. Such an effort ends in complete discouragement. It begins with an excessive enthusiasm and constructs an autonomous humanism that makes the human being the measure of all things. But when the results prove pitifully small, when all the encouraging technological progress produces a weapon capable of destroying humankind in an instant, then we are attacked by fear and discouragement, we are tempted to nihilism and, inevitably, to suicide.

The other attitude is the attitude of faith: to "rely on" the Other, the Absolute, who comes to us and offers his help. To believe is to share in the solidity of God. The believer must begin by acknowledging his weakness, his radical inability to get himself out of the state that raises so many questions in his mind. He must trust the "Other" and throw himself into the void; he must count to ten and hope that the parachute will open. Faith supposes a total trust in the Absolute who promises his support; he must be answered with unlimited confidence. We give our trust while we are still in the condition that causes us so much anxiety, for the state of anxiety is connatural even for the believer. Faith does not rid us of the anxiety; it simply gives us hope. The anxiety is no longer turned in on itself so that it must inevitably consume the person. But it is a mistake to think that a believer is without worries, and that he has everything worked out like a mathematical theorem. Any such state can only be a mirage.

The essential attitude of the Christian requires, then, that he be constantly taking the leap out of his own nothingness, which he magnanimously acknowledges, into the stability of the divine being. It would be a mistake, however, to think that the other end of the leap is somewhere in our present life. The Christian's great temptation is the one Peter experienced on Mount Tabor: "Let us set up three tents here"; that is, let us make our dwelling in the comfortable, secure routine of a utilitarian religion.

No! The Christian in this life is at war; he must continually struggle. The leap of faith is not a leap of escape and flight, but a leap in which he lands ever anew on the paths which together make up the broad highway of history.

SPLENDID RISK

The great third-century Christian writer, Clement of Alexandria, describes the Christian life in a phrase whose full overtones cannot readily be captured in translation: "What a splendid risk, to pass freely over into God's camp!"[12] Clement is using a technical expression referring to a man in military service who abandons the ranks in which he has been fighting and passes over to the enemy.

Such a step is risky indeed, for there are two adversaries on the scene, and each of them wants to monopolize the services and homage of the men who make up the armies. In a similar way, the person who would reach God must start from within a hostile army, and, if he takes the step, he must be aware of the risks it involves. But that is precisely what faith is. Faith is not—as we have said so often now—a merely intellectual acceptance of an abstract scheme of dogmatic and moral truths that someone proposes to us. Faith is something that involves and compels the whole person.

The believer must begin by cutting his own roots and launching himself out into the void while tightly enclosed as it were in the space capsule of faith that he himself must steer. It is true enough that the initiative belongs to God who, from a divine platform, catapults the believer far out of his native atmosphere. But once in orbit the believer cannot be satisfied to be comfortably guided from afar by a launching station on the solid earth.

It is this very combination of divine initiative and human collaboration that gives rise to the risk which is unavoidable in the religious adventure of passing over into the ranks of God.

The risk can be avoided in two ways. One is to stay in the army in which one finds oneself. Not to dare desert, and even to try to defend one's position with seemingly valid reasons. Why abandon the tents of the human encampment and get lost in the fantasy world of a paradise that is the product of fear and ambition?

The other and more cynical way of avoiding the risk is to think that the new Lord whom we aim to serve must fulfill all our aspirations as a reward for our heroic act of desertion. This is to believe that heroism is a once-and-for-all act and that we can immediately send in our bill for a high reward to the person who accepted our enlistment.

But this second way does not represent faith. Faith is not an insurance policy that exempts us from constantly facing risk. Faith is risk, and nothing else. But it is the most splendid of risks.

THE SUN SETS MORE QUICKLY NOW

The felt absence of God has become a pathological condition among our contemporaries. In the long run, that is reason for optimism and hope.

The people of the Enlightenment were still living on the spiritual heritage of European Christianity and therefore could be casual and superficial in their handling of the religious problem. They could joke about the divine and engage in a lot of clever conceptual fencing with it. Atheism and irreligion had become fashionable and could go around boasting of their own daring, but they did it in a frivolous and shallow way.

The modern person is much more serious, and the discovery of God's absence fills him with fear and trembling. Having dislodged God from the center of his intellectual world he now confronts a dizzyingly unknown and insubstantial world. He claims he can do without God but he is filled with a deep nostalgia for God's presence. He longs for God with anxious humility, often without being aware of the fact.

The moment has come, therefore, to begin again the search for God. Never before has it been so urgently necessary to speak to our wearied contemporaries of prayer. Prayer is an attitude that springs from human nature itself, and a philosopher like Gabriel Marcel can consider the treatment of prayer to be an essential part of his existential metaphysics.[13]

Prayer has always been necessary, but in past ages life unfolded according to a much slower rhythm and a person could store up for himself the means of future nourishment. Thus the education acquired in youth remained valid throughout almost the whole of life, for in any one person's lifetime the human race itself did not notably advance in its understanding of reality. The same was true of the spiritual life; God adapted himself to our circumstances and manifested himself as the rhythm of human life suggested.

On the other hand, the first cosmonaut told us that in his swift flight around the earth he saw the sun set every ninety minutes. Something similar is happening today in the life of the spirit: God is appearing more frequently on the horizon of the religious person's life. Therefore prayer must be thought of as an attitude rather than as an individual act. The dark nights that formerly were experienced only by a chosen few are today descending upon a broad spectrum of believers. God manifests himself to us with greater frequency because the rhythm of our lives has been speeded up.

Genuine believers must be prepared to accept the fact that God's paradoxical action is to be forced upon them more often. The fact is, indeed, a sign of predilection. It does not matter that God's absence should wrench from our anguished hearts the rending cry of helplessness: "My God, my God, why have you forsaken me?" For it is the paradoxical abandonment of God's own Son that assures us of God's permanent presence in the wide world of human anguish.

In Germany today life has become almost totally mechanized. For most things people do not have to go to a store and talk to a clerk who will show them various goods and provide what is wanted. They need only go to one of the many vending machines, put in the correct amount of money, and pull out a drawer. There in the drawer is the object they want. Of course, sometimes the money inserted is not the right amount; then the robot clerk politely returns it to them.

We often come to God with complaints and demands. We think there can be no reason why he should not hear our prayers; we even come to him with a proud list of our merits: our religious background, our acts of worship, our financial contributions to charitable undertakings, our collaboration in apostolic enterprises. But God remains silent; like the German vending machine he returns our money to us. We leave the church with our own wretched resources that were not enough to buy the favor we wanted.

Foreigners are often naive enough to put the money of their own country into the slot in the vending machine; their money sounds the same on paper as the German, but it is in fact worthless. It's no use; the machine carefully returns their money to them. German merchandise can be bought only with German money.

In like fashion we have tried to buy God's favor with our pitiful human money. The result is that at the end of our proud pseudo-prayer we're left with our money in our hand and are further from God than when we started to pray.

It takes divine money to buy divine gifts, and that money is faith. The first thing we must do is to let God, who has the initiative in the religious life, take possession of us. We must give God full scope when it comes to shaping our lives.

God does not destroy our freedom, far from it. In fact, the greatest mystery of all is the immense respect he shows for this freedom. But we can *freely allow* God to take all the initiative. Only then does the machine for producing grace operate properly. Our human money is taken up and ennobled by God and is changed into the currency that can buy human fulfillment. That fulfillment, hidden though it is from us in a luminous darkness, is promised us by the faith we profess.

NOTES

1. Cf. the rabbinic texts in Joseph Bonsirven, S.J., *Le judaïsme palestinien au temps de Jésus-Christ: Sa théologie,* 2 vols. (Paris: Beauchesne, 1935), 1:250–54.

2. Ibid., 2:320–21.

3. Géza Vermèx, *Discovery in the Judean Desert* (New York: Desclee, 1956), pp. 112–13.

4. Buber, *Eclipse of God,* p. 69.

5. Camus, *The Rebel,* p. 68.

6. Albert Gelin, "La foi dans l'Ancien Testament," *Lumière et Vie,* no. 22 (1955):433.

7. Cf. Michel Testuz, *Les idées religieuses du Livre des Jubilés* (Geneva: Droz, 1960), p. 7.

8. "The Book of Jubilees," trans. R.H. Charles, in *The Apocrypha and Pseudepigrapha of the Old Testament in English,* ed. R.H. Charles, 2 vols. (Oxford: Clarendon Press, 1913), 2:30.

9. Ibid., p. 31.

10. Cf. Franz J. Leenhardt, *The Epistle to the Romans: A Commentary,* trans. Harold Knight (Cleveland: World, 1961), p. 120.

11. Cf. The Council of Trent, "Decree on Justification," c. 7; text in *The Church Teaches: Documents of the Church in English Translation,* ed. and trans. John F. Clarkson, S.J., et al. (St. Louis: B. Herder, 1955), pp. 234–35, no. 564.

12. Clement of Alexandria, *Protrepticus* [Exhortation (to the Greeks)] X, 93, 2.

13. Gabriel Marcel, *The Mystery of Being,* trans. René Hague (Chicago: Regnery, 1951), vol. 2, ch. 6.

CHAPTER 5

CHRISTIANITY IS OTHER PEOPLE

CHRISTIAN MORALITY
IS A MORALITY OF BROTHERLY LOVE

On a few occasions the synoptic Gospels use almost identical language in reporting the clear and unequivocal teaching of Jesus. On one such occasion the Jewish intellectual class asks the Master a very important question: What does he consider to be the primary content of the moral law? (cf. Luke 10:25–37; Mark 12:28–34; Matt. 22:35–40).

"The law and the prophets" (Matt. 22:40) was a stereotyped expression meaning the whole content of revealed moral teaching. Jesus does not claim to provide a new moral teaching in addition to that which God had revealed in earlier times. On the contrary, the "morality of love" had already found explicit formulation in the book of Deuteronomy. The Jewish lawyers expressly recognize this fact:

On one occasion a lawyer stood up to pose him this problem: "Teacher, what must I do to inherit everlasting life?" Jesus answered him: "What is written in the law? How do you read it?" He replied: "You shall love the Lord your God with all your heart, with all your soul, with all your strength, and with all your mind; and your neighbor as yourself." Jesus said, "You have answered correctly. Do this and you shall live" [Luke 10:25–28].

Matthew puts on Jesus' lips a value judgment about the commandment of love:

Jesus said to him: " 'You shall love the Lord your God with your whole heart, with your whole soul, and with all your mind.' This is the greatest and first commandment. The second is like it: 'You shall love your neighbor as yourself.' On these two commandments the whole law is based, and the prophets as well" [Matt. 22:37–40].

On this point Paul follows the synoptic tradition and also offers a penetrating explanation of the moral importance of brotherly love:

He who loves his neighbor has fulfilled the law. The commandments, "You shall not commit adultery; you shall not murder; you shall not steal; you shall not covet," and any other commandments there may be are all summed up in this, "You shall love your neighbor as yourself." Love never does any wrong to the neighbor, hence love is the fulfillment of the law [Rom. 13:8–10].

Paul is here saying that the fulfillment of any divine precept includes a formal act of love of neighbor, and, conversely, that if a person is serious about practicing brotherly love in an unlimited way, he will obey each and every commandment of the law. Chapter 13 of the First Epistle to the Corinthians gives a complete list of the virtues, and Paul can say of each: Love is, or love does, or love does not.

Rather than engage in an abstract analysis of Pauline teaching on Christian morality as morality of love, we shall listen to one of his exhortations and see how his preaching is wholly focused on the basic theme of love.

Paul writes to the Christian community of Galatia:

My brothers, remember that you have been called to live in freedom—but not a freedom that gives free rein to the flesh. Out of love place yourselves at one another's service. The whole law has found its fulfillment in this one saying: "You shall love your neighbor as yourself" [Gal. 5:13–14].

The Apostle then proceeds in a way that is consistent with this basic statement. The whole subsequent exhortation, which presents a complete outline of moral conduct for the Christians of Galatia, is based on the presupposition of brotherly love.

Brotherly love is so essential for the Church that without it the very existence of the Church is threatened: "If you go on biting and tearing one another to pieces, take care! You will end up in mutual destruction!'' (Gal. 5:15). The Christian community is responsible for its own unity and thereby for its own existence. In his penetrating analysis Paul seems to be anticipating future weakenings of the Church's unity, all of which will be due much more to the lack of brotherly love within the community than to attacks from outside.

Paul then goes on to explain his morality of love. He begins by setting forth a general principle: ''My point is that you should live in accord with the spirit and you will not yield to the cravings of the flesh'' (Gal. 5:16). He is not thinking here of any dualism within the person, as if one part were in physical and moral conflict with the other. He is thinking rather of two different historical situations, each of which affects the whole person. The person-as-flesh is left to his own resources, attempting nonetheless to carry out the plan of God that is made known in the law. The person-as-spirit, on the other hand, is the believer who has acknowledged his own helplessness and allowed the divine Spirit to make his dwelling within him.

The cravings of the flesh have a sad ending: Instead of loving God and neighbor, a person loves himself in a disordered way and is subject to all the evils described in verses 19–21. That is what the person-as-flesh makes of himself.

Still speaking in specific terms, the Apostle goes on to list ''what proceeds from the flesh,'' that is, what the person-as-flesh, left to his own resources, can accomplish. Paul speaks of what proceeds from the flesh as ''works,'' thus emphasizing freshly our proud determination to live by our own powers. But he speaks of the outcome of the Spirit's presence as ''fruit,'' a word that in the New Testament expresses the idea of a striking, unexpected, spontaneous manifestation of life.

There is no need, says the Apostle, to search very deeply in order to find out what the self-sufficient efforts of the person-as-flesh lead to: ''It is obvious what proceeds from the flesh'' (Gal. 5:19). Paul is usually very pessimistic about the moral situation of the contemporary world,[1] and even his exhortations to new Christians suppose that their Christian moral life had begun with a leap out of a very corrupt way of life. The list of vices that Paul gives here in Galatians is not meant to be complete. The emphasis is on faults against brotherly love (hostilities, bickering, jealousy, outbursts of rage, selfish rivalries, dissensions, factions, envy); sexual misbehavior is not the center of concern and is described only in general terms (lewd conduct, impurity, licentiousness).

The Apostle then goes on to describe the "fruit" of the Spirit. The person who is in Christ and possesses the Spirit of God is now empowered to achieve the human ideal that the law presents as the aim of human conduct and indeed of our very existence. The enumeration of the virtues that are the "fruit" of the Spirit is likewise not intended to be complete; moreover it does not refer solely to some Christian elite, but has in mind the daily reality of every believer's life.

"Love" refers chiefly to brotherly love. The list of virtues, like the list of vices, is drawn up with the social life of the community in mind. Paul mentions love first, because it is the foundation on which all other authentic manifestations of the Spirit are built.

"Joy" is a typically messianic concept which the Bible regards as a sign of the future age. In the Gospels, including John, joy is a messianic concept and closely connected with the idea of the kingdom of God: "Come, share your master's joy!" (Matt. 25:21–23).

For Paul, joy also has a social function: It is the sign of communion among the members of Christ's body. Joy is, as it were, a wholesome juice that has a life-giving effect due to the constant process of symbiosis that goes on among the members of the body of Christ. Joy runs from Paul to the faithful and from the faithful to Paul; it makes up for deficiencies, balances differences, and expands the Church's life. Paul can therefore say that "I know you all well enough to be convinced that my happiness is yours" (2 Cor. 2:3); that "in the midst of severe trial their [the Churches of Macedonia] overflowing joy and deep poverty have produced an abundant generosity" (2 Cor. 8:2); that his return to Philippi will be "for your joy and your progress in the faith," so that "my being with you once again should make you even prouder of me in Christ" (Phil. 1:25–26); and that the Philippians, after receiving joy from Paul, should in turn "make my joy complete" (Phil. 2:2).

"Peace" means primarily the peace that exists between

brothers and sisters in community. It is based on the peace that God establishes with people in Jesus Christ (Rom. 5:7) and which he gives to his people (Gal. 6:16). In Rom. 14:17 joy and peace appear side by side as elements in the cohesiveness of the community.

"Patient endurance" is applied in the New Testament chiefly to God (cf. Luke 18:7; Rom. 2:4; 9:22; 1 Pet. 3:20; 2 Pet. 3:9–15) and describes the unexpected mercy of God who, instead of punishing the sinner, bestows grace upon him. But God wishes the pardoned person to show the same understanding to his brothers and sisters (Matt. 18:32–33; Rom. 2:3–4; Eph. 4:2–3; 2 Cor. 6:6; 1 Cor. 13:4).

"Kindness" is the crown of "generosity" and, perhaps for that reason, is listed after "generosity" in some manuscripts of the Vulgate.

"Generosity" is that heartfelt unselfishness that offers help in every useful work (Rom. 15:14; 2 Thes. 1:11; Eph. 5:9).

"Faith" (pistis), in this context, cannot be theological faith, but means fidelity or devotion to one's neighbor (Rom. 3:3; 1 Cor. 13:7).

"Mildness" means the renunciation of anger and violence; in addition, as used in the New Testament and the Septuagint, the word carries a weight of meaning that is derived from the concepts of the 'anaw and the 'ani of the Hebrew Old Testament.

Finally "chastity" is understood not solely as self-control (as it is in a gnostic type of moral solipsism), but as a means of fostering community life, since the "repression" of egotistic instincts makes it easier for the members of Christ's body to enter into communion with one another.

After describing the "fruit of the Spirit" (an authentic morality of brotherly love), Paul goes on to exhort his readers to build up the unity of the group, since the attacks of the Galatian agitators were aimed chiefly at breaking up the compact, unified community which the Apostle had formed (Gal. 5:26–6:9).

While not naming his opponents and even including himself among the potential sinners, Paul exhorts his readers: "Let us never be boastful" (Gal. 5:26). He is referring to an inversion of values when it comes to building up the Church: Instead of looking only for the most effective way to build it up, a person tries to use the Church to show off the builder's supposed talents. The false apostle, who substitutes a morality based on egotism for the morality based on brotherly love, aims only at displaying himself. To achieve his purposes he does not hesitate even to "challenge" others and to create opposing camps so that he may profit by the division. The resultant civil war within the community gives rise to "jealousy," the legitimate offspring of the unscrupulous quest for personal conquest.

We have no exact knowledge of the internal state of the church in Galatia, but Paul's exhortations to mutual esteem allow us to glimpse the essential lines of the situation. The exhortation is concerned basically with "fraternal correction" or "ministry of reprimand," which is exercised chiefly when the people are gathered for worship. The Apostle says that even if a Christian "is detected in sin" (Gal. 6:1), the reprimand should be given in a gentle and loving way. Those "who live by the spirit," to whom this exhortation is directed, are probably not some superior class of Christians but all Christians, since all (as the whole Epistle keeps insisting) possess the Spirit and are therefore able to live according to the Spirit.

We may also suspect that those who are reprimanded are the catechumens or candidates for baptism. Mature Christians, who already possess the Spirit through baptism, must have shown uncalled-for superiority and rigor to those they were instructing. Paul exhorts instructors to give their reprimands in a constructive way: "Gently set him right." This kind of gentleness is based on humility with regard to one's own faith: "each of you trying to avoid falling into temptation himself." The catechist may possess the Spirit but he is not confirmed in grace, and must himself make decision after decision as he gradually achieves that full existence that he can reach with the Spirit's help. No Christian, therefore, however high his rank in the government of the Church, can hurl harsh anathemas from the supposedly secure heights of doctrine.

Quite the contrary, for brotherly love requires the members of the community to be ready to "carry one another's burdens" (Gal. 6:2). The "burden" of which the Apostle is speaking includes the difficulties of life, the sense of faults committed, the vices whose foremost victim is the guilty person himself, and the temperament which weigh upon us. In the present co seems to mean by "burden" chiefly moral faults, as temptations and remorse that precede and follow such faults.

Therefore the instructor who sees before him a poor sinner, bent under the weight of his moral wretchedness, must respond with loving care and try to lighten his burden. A severe reprimand would only lay an even heavier weight on the person's shoulders, one that might crush him completely. The instructor must, then, hasten to take on himself his brother's "burden."

St. Ignatius of Antioch uses the same Greek verb *bastazo* (carry), when he urges Bishop Polycarp in the exercise of his high hierarchic office to act as one who would lighten the burdens of the faithful: "Bear with all just as the Lord does with you. Have patience with all in charity."[2] Only in this way will the Galatians "fulfill the law of Christ," which, as the Apostle has just pointed out (Gal. 5:14), is reducible to brotherly love.

The Christian who does not love his brothers and show it in mercy to the fallen, "thinks he amounts to something, when in fact he is nothing" (Gal. 6:3).

The source of this kind of pride which the Apostle must reprove is a person's belief in his own spiritual superiority over the sinner to be corrected. This is the attitude of the Pharisee in Luke's Gospel (18:9–14), a sadistic pleasure in the sin of another because one's own supposedly impeccable and luminous conduct stands out the better against such a dark background.

Paul takes quite a different view of the situation and exhorts his reader to examine his own conduct and not to indulge in this kind of proud comparison with the defects of others: "Each man should look to his conduct; if he has reason to boast of anything, it will be because the achievement is his and not another's" (Gal. 6:4).

The Christian must thus sincerely examine his conscience with a view to God's judgment; before God "everyone should bear his own responsibility" (6:5). The standard applied by the divine Judge is absolute, not relative. He will not reward the one who shows himself superior to his neighbor on various points, but rather him who orders his affairs according to the norm of divine judgment, which is brotherly love.

After listening to Paul's sermon to certain severe Christians of Galatia, we shall surely find much to change in both the content and the style of our own preaching, or private exhortations, and perhaps our manuals of moral theology.

THE CHURCH OF LOVE

Love is so essential for the Church that Paul even uses "love" as a name for the community. One of the ways in which he speaks of Christians as a group is by the term *agape* or "love."[3]

In the second generation the Pauline usage would become part of everyday Christian language. Thus St. Ignatius of Antioch would address his letters to "the Agape of Rome," "the Agape of Ephesus," etc.

We may well ask ourselves today: Can our present-day "churches," our "Christian" temples, rightly be called "dwellings of brotherly love"?

People have always made the foolish attempt to enclose God within the narrow limits of a temple made to our own measure. It seems as though God's omnipresence, his entering into the depths of the individual's only existence, would be too disturbing. Therefore God is confined to the temple and kept in his place by the great vaults and the rich ornamentation of worship. People come to the temple to give "god" all kinds of gifts and to offer their pleas and promises, so that they may meet him comfortably in his dark niche and he may not think of leaving the sacred precincts and forcing his way into our secular lives where he would only upset and disturb our consciences.

Within the temple, too—but only there—the prophets and the dervishes can play their cloying melodies and with their sticky sermons bring a delightful thrill to a few egotistic and self-satisfied believers. These devout faithful are constantly thanking God for having given them shelter under the welcoming arches of the temple while outside the wicked and the foolish rave and howl.

Such was the attitude of the Jews at that crucial moment in Jesus' virile preaching when he said: "You will find your temple deserted" (Matt. 23:38).

Jesus rarely preached in the Temple or even in the synagogues.

At the end of his life he was officially excommunicated from the synagogue and had to carry on his preaching at the crossroads, on the routes of the endless caravans, on lakeshores and riverbanks, aboard the boats of humble fishermen, or at the table of some kindly tax-gatherer. In the Temple there was too much egotism and pride, and the men of the Temple banished God because he spoke too much of brotherly love and humble detachment.

Rabindranath Tagore has given beautiful expression to this thought in his poem, *The Harvest.*

"Lord," said a servant to the king, "the holy man Narottam never enters your royal temple. If you were to go to the grove along the road, you would see people hastening there to hear him sing the praises of God, as the bees swarm about the white lotus. But meanwhile the temple stands empty, and no one fills the golden honey jar!"

The king, humiliated in his heart, went to the field where Narottam was sitting in the grass and praying, and he said to him: "My father, why do you sit here in the dust of the field, in order to preach the love of God, instead of going to the temple with the golden dome?"

"Because God is not in your temple," Narottam answered.

The king was angered and said: "Don't you realize that twenty million pieces of gold went into putting up that splendid building and it was consecrated with very costly rites?"

"Yes, I realize that," said Narottam. "That was the year in which fire destroyed your town, and thousands of poor people knocked in vain at your door. Then God said: 'This wretched fellow will not provide his brothers with a roof, yet he wants to put one up for me!' And so God went out to stay with the destitute, under the trees along the road.

"All that golden pomp you speak of is as empty within as the hot breath of your own pride."

The king was enraged and shouted at him: "Leave my kingdom!"

The holy man answered him peacefully: "You are but exiling me from the land whence you have already exiled my God."

Tagore is right.

With less of the lush Eastern style but perhaps with greater poetic realism, a Christian of our own day has written: "I went out looking for a church that might be open for prayer, but I found none. Then I decided to take a walk and try to pray as I went about the city. In the streets it was cold and drizzling. The whole place was like a huge dark church, and the saints therein were the poor tired women selling chestnuts in dirty little wooden kiosks.''

We are outraged when people burn and destroy our magnificent churches, but we rarely reflect that we, the so-called Christians, have already profaned the sanctuary with ''the hot breath of our pride'' and the disgusting spittle of our own egotism. We have banished God from our churches.

On Holy Thursday we sing a beautiful medieval song with a refrain that runs: ''Where charity and love prevail, there God is ever found.'' On the day when the thuribles spread the sweet fragrance of brotherly love in our churches, the latter will never again be threatened with arson. But until that happens we run the risk of reducing our religion to a mere hobby. This explains why, when religion is accepted by a society that is self-satisfied and really indifferent to genuine religion, it is because religion is taken simply as a pretty little relic of the past.

There are societies today that even call themselves Christian and boast publicly that they are rooted in a glorious Christian civilization. They try to convince themselves that this rich religious inheritance commands their every action and puts its seal on it. But as Pius XI pointed out in his courageous encyclical against German Nazism: It is not enough to make fine rhetorical use of God's name while cynically trampling on his commandments.

These hypocritically Christian societies are, in practice, the least tolerant of authentic religious impulses. On the other hand, a Christianity that remains purely cultic and hieratic is not only tolerated; it is eagerly protected, since behind the thick curtain of incense a multitude of motives may be hidden that people dare not openly admit to.

The priest is asked to bless new homes and factories and businesses. But he is not allowed to remind people publicly of evangelical morality, the morality of brotherly love, with its heart-piercing simplicity. If courageous preachers appear, people hypocritically rend their garments, attack them, and heap nonsensical insults upon them.

In short, these societies have room for the priest and levite who are content with their incense-perfumed hands and pass by the wounded man on the road from Jerusalem to Jericho. Then they have to play down the value of the good Samaritan's action by calling it philanthropy or secular humanism, even though Jesus saw in the Samaritan's action a perfect example of that charity, or love of neighbor, which is the heart of his message.

The absence of brotherly love that characterizes so many societies and institutions which claim to be Christian often shows itself in the discomfort people feel when confronted with the transcendent. The discomfort manifests itself in the sacrilegious effort to cut God down to the size of our narrow intellects. It also shows in the bold claim that we can imagine and communicate to others all the realities that form a constellation around the transcendent One, and that we can do so by using norms derived from the workings of a society which we have invented and brought into being for our own use. "Responsibility for this state of affairs lies with the pharisaism that has emasculated Christian ethics and confused the morality of bourgeois society with the gospel teaching on salvation."[4]

Bernanos makes the same point in a more concrete way in one of his sharp invectives against "Christian" Pharisees:

And what have you laymen made of hell? A kind of penal servitude for eternity, on the lines of your convict prisons on earth, to which you condemn in advance all the wretched felons your police have hunted from the beginning—"enemies of society," as you call them. You're kind enough to include the blasphemers and the profane. What proud or reasonable man could stomach such a notion of God's justice? . . . Hell is judged by the standards of the world, and hell is not of this world.[5]

That puts it perfectly: Hell is not of this world. Christ warned us not to make the great mistake and commit the great injustice of condemning others. "The Father himself judges no one, but has assigned all judgment to the Son" (John 5:22). Perhaps the only exception to that rule is the act of judging itself: "If you do not forgive others, neither will your Father forgive you" (Matt. 6:15). We can never know the outcome of each individual's final mysterious encounter with God, in which the divine judgment takes place. But if there is a norm to keep in mind, it is the one Christ himself has given us: Hell will be the native place of those who dare condemn others.

It required a great deal of effort for the stern command against condemning others to make its way into the early Christian communities. Chapter eight of the fourth Gospel, which contains the account of Jesus pardoning the adulterous woman, is missing from many ancient manuscripts, a fact which raised questions about its authenticity. Today impartial critics agree in assigning the narrative to John. Its absence from many early texts of the Gospel is easily explained by the fact that many Christian communities followed a very rigid penitential discipline for adultery and like sins, and that consequently the reading of this part of the Gospel became a source of pharisaic scandal.

Let us, therefore, not be guilty of immense stupidity and injustice by peopling hell with our candidates. Let us rather leave judgment to the Son of God, for hell is not of this world.

Fortunately, the more flourishing Christian societies of the present day are showing a sincere desire for renewal and for a return to the authentic Christian morality of brotherly love.

In working for the union of all Christians, we often forget that love (even in its ideological context) is the only force that can lead to an integration of the churches. "Where charity and love prevail, there God is ever found."

NOTES

1. Cf. Rom. 1:18–32; 1 Cor. 5:9–10; 6:12–20; Eph. 4:17–19; Col. 3:5–11; 1 Thess. 4:6; 1 Tim. 1:9–11.

2. St. Ignatius of Antioch, "Letter to Polycarp," trans. James J. Kleist, S.J., in *The Epistles of St. Clement of Rome and St. Ignatius of Antioch,* Ancient Christian Writers 1 (Westminster, Md.: Newman, 1946), p. 96.

3. Cf. José María González-Ruiz, "Sentido comunitario-eclesial de algunos sustantivos abstractos en San Pablo," in *Sacra Pagina: Miscellanea Biblica Congressus Internationalis Catholici de Re Biblica,* ed. J. Coppens, A. Descamps, and E. Massaux (Paris: Gabalda, 1959), 2:322–26.

4. Albérès, *Rebelión de los escritores,* p. 69.

5. Georges Bernanos, *Diary of a Country Priest,* trans. Pamela Morris (New York: Macmillan, 1937), p. 163.

CHAPTER 6

OBJECT OF BROTHERLY LOVE: THE WHOLE PERSON AND EVERY PERSON

Marxists reproach Christians for being narrow when it comes to love. "Religious love," as the Marxists see it, is bestowed only on an abstraction: the soul.

Our purpose in this chapter is to use biblical anthropology in order to describe the person, our "neighbor," the one we are ordered to love in the first and foremost commandment of revealed ethics.

THE PERSON IN THE BIBLE

It is not easy to give a clear outline of Israelite anthropology. Semitic thought is much more elusive and hazy in outline than the mental categories to which the West is used, for the latter have their origin in the tidiness, clarity, and sense of proportion of the Greek mind.

If we are to gain any understanding of biblical thought on our present subject we must take a bird's-eye view and be satisfied with a handful of conclusions reached by scholarly analysis, even though these conclusions are not always entirely consistent with one another. This, at any rate, is the approach we shall take to the immense field of biblical anthropology, in an effort to gather its more representative statements concerning the person and to put together a loose descriptive definition of him.

To begin with, the person is flesh. The English word "flesh" stands for the Hebrew *basar*, but the English concept and term are far from capturing the meaning of the biblical word.

In Hebrew, as in Arabic, *basar* may originally have meant the skin, the covering of the human body. Later on it came to mean the whole body (1 Kings 21:27; 2 Kings 6:30; Job 4:15; Prov. 4:22). But body-flesh is the seat not only of the fleshly or material powers of the person, but of his spiritual aspirations as well. Thus, for example, the flesh is pierced by desire for God (Ps. 84:3); it is capable of spiritual joy (Ps. 16:9) and of fear (Ps. 119:120). On the other hand, the idea that the flesh is the source or seat of sin is wholly alien to the Old Testament.[1]

When "flesh" is set over against "spirit" in the Old Testament, there is no question (as in the Greek dichotomy) of a civil war within the person, but simply of two aspects that are extrinsic to each other. "Flesh" means the person insofar as he is a fragile being, subject to decay and destined some day to break up. "Spirit," on the contrary, is a kind of current of vitality and fulness that has its origin in God and animates all the beings that make up creation. "Spirit" (the Hebrew *ru'ah*) is the beneficent "breath" of God that permeates creation and gives existence and life to all beings. "If you hide your face, they are dismayed; if you take away their breath, they perish and return to their dust. When you send forth your spirit, they are created, and you renew the face of the earth" (Ps. 104:29–30).

Thus the dualism of matter and spirit plays no part in the usual biblical antithesis of flesh and spirit. Flesh is opposed to spirit as weakness to strength, as the fragile to the solidly established, and as what is mortal to what lives forever.[2]

"Flesh," then, expresses a complete and integrated conception of the person, embracing the whole person and every person. Every person is flesh, and the whole person is flesh. The person—the historical person, who actually exists—is a being-for-death. He can find nothing within himself on which to ground himself solidly. He is an essentially dependent being who must derive his existence from another.

The "other" is God, the being who enjoys full and eternal life and whose ground is in himself. "Spirit," conceived naively as a life-giving breath, is a current of energy that originates in God and sustains the creature in existence. The Israelites did not push the analysis any further nor shift out of the realm of imprecise metaphor. They never attempted a philosophical synthesis with clearly defined concepts. Thus the very concept of matter is notable for its absence from the biblical literature of both Testaments. Even when the name "Spirit" is applied to God, the point is not that he is a being without any admixture of matter (which is what "spiritual" means according to our Greek conceptual categories). When the Bible calls God Spirit, it means that he is Plenitude, Strength, Life. Over against this God who is Spirit stand creatures, all of whom (including human beings) are of themselves only flesh; that is, their existence is mediated, fragile, easily disrupted. But creatures can share in the divine "spirit" and thus remain in existence.

This situation explains why in biblical thought there is a close union between the cosmic and the religious. Religion in its literal sense is a "binding" or "connecting," and, when taken in this way, determines the very existence of the creature. The more religious a creature is, that is, the more connected with or united to God it is, the more fully and stably it will share in the divine being, and thus will be the more fully itself.

This explains why life was regarded as a gift of God, a grace which he grants, out of his own fullness of being, to those who love and obey him. It also explains the belief ordinarily found in the Old Testament writings that a person receives his reward from God during the present life and that the reward of the just consists in a long life. We can understand, then, the dismay caused by the premature and violent death of a just person, for it seemed to justify doubts about the justice of God.

Under the influence of this difficulty, Israelite thought gradually developed a belief in a future resurrection as the way in which the "living God" (Num. 14:28; 2 Kings 2:2; Jer. 10:10; Ezek. 20:31; 33:11) would assert himself over "the powers of death" and "sheol." Earlier times, in fact, had already spoken of two men who had avoided the powerful hand of death: Enoch, who God "took" in reward for his piety, since he had "walked with God" (Gen. 5:24), and the prophet Elijah, prototype of justice and integrity (2

Kings 2:1–11). Yahweh, the "living God," could not be limited by death in his creative, life-giving action, and he showed this power from time to time by calling the dead back to life. The Old Testament relates three cases of resuscitation (1 Kings 17:22; 2 Kings 4:31–37; 13:21); in all three instances Yahweh himself restores life to corpses, the prophet acting merely as Yahweh's instrument (1 Kings 17:21).

The idea of the resurrection of the people as a people was already familiar (cf. Hos. 6:1–2). But a new importance attaches to chapter 37 of Ezekiel because it seems to speak not only of the resurrection of the people as a society but of a resurrection of the dead themselves. The question, "Son of man, can these bones come to life?" (Ezek. 37:3), indicates that people had doubts that had been completely eliminated when the issue was the resurrection of the nation as a nation. Moreover, the dead in question are called "these slain" (37:9); the viewpoint seems to be that of Daniel at a later time, when he speaks of the martyrs as the first to benefit from the resurrection.[3]

The idea of David restored to life, which we meet in Ezekiel 34:23 and 37:24, seems to point to a resurrection of the king by way of anticipation of a resurrection of the masses of people.

The death-resurrection sequence makes its appearance in connection with the Servant of Yahweh, especially in the long confession that begins in Isaiah 53:4: "While we thought of him as stricken. . . . " But the resurrection of the Servant was also thought of as something extraordinary, something that could happen only by way of exception to an individual. However, all of God's extraordinary interventions in the Old Testament, such as prophecy, priesthood, and election, tend to become universalized.[4] Thus the hope of resurrection gradually embraced the mass of the people, especially since it seemed to be the only answer to the problem of retribution and to the increasingly critical questions raised against the doctrine of rewards and punishments. Resurrection, as the answer to this problem and these questions, would finally become an accepted dogma, as we can see in 2 Maccabees 7:23 and Daniel 12.

As these brief remarks on biblical anthropology have brought out, the person was always thought of as a single, unified being;

nowhere does the Bible entertain the idea of full life beyond death and its corruption.

It is true enough that the Israelites believed in a survival after death, in the region of Sheol or realm of the dead. But the life the dead lived there was shadowy and insubstantial. Death was conceived of as a state in which one's vital powers were reduced to a minimum. The state there is like unconsciousness or sleep (Job 14:10–12); it lacks the bonds of community that are characteristic of living persons (14:21–22); the dead person is alone. Weakness, then, is the distinctive mark of those who dwell in Sheol. Even the *rephaim,* who are the aristocracy of the realm of the dead, are now weak beings who have lost the immense power they once had as divine helpers.[5]

Emphasis on death as separation from God could, of itself, have led to dualist solutions, but faith in the omnipotence of Yahweh was so strong that it rendered such solutions impossible. Thus we find firm statements that even Sheol was completely subject to the power of God:

"It is Yahweh who causes men to die and to live, who sends down to *Sheol* and recalls thence," sings the author of the song of Hannah (1 Sam. 2:6) and for Amos Yahweh's omnipotence does not stop at the gates of *Sheol* (Amos 9:2). Life and death are within Yahweh's power, but since Yahweh's power was the sovereignty of a living God, death could not manifest itself to the same degree as life. Despite Yahweh's dominion over the world of the dead, there is always some incompatibility between him and death; that is why the solution of the problem of death could only be found in the final triumph of life.[6]

Robert Martin-Achard writes:

Before the Fall, between Adam and death, which is part of his natural lot as an element in his human heritage, there stands the Living God; His presence is sufficient to ward off death . . . of whose imminence he [Adam] is constantly reminded by the enmity he encounters everywhere on his way, in the world (Gen. 3:15), in his home (Gen. 3:16), and in his work (Gen. 3:17ff.). . . . Man, then, is born mortal, but by his sin he renders death effective; it enters as a reality into his existence; henceforth he lives as one who has heard the capital sentence pronounced against him. He is aware that death is at hand and he cannot escape it. Between the presence of God and the presence of death he has chosen the latter. By his disobedience Adam has transformed the human situation into a curse; in this sense, death, through the threatening shadow it constantly throws on his life, is truly the wages of sin. Thus, accidentally, man becomes that "being-for-death" that is at the core of Heidegger's thought.[7]

It is perfectly understandable, then, that the desire for death should have no place in the ascetical and moral world of the pious Israelite. Since life is the supreme good, the desire for death can only come as the crowning moment of despair or discouragement (cf. 2 Sam. 1:9; 1 Kings 19:4–5; Hos. 10:8; Jer. 8:3; Job 3:21; Ecclus. 40:1–15). Wretched though it may be, life is better than death: "Indeed, for any among the living there is hope; a live dog is better off than a dead lion. For the living know that they are to die, but the dead no longer know anything" (Eccles. 9:4–5). We must wait for the period of the Maccabees to meet the idea (common among the Greeks) that a glorious death in battle is to be preferred to a shameful flight (2 Macc. 8:10). Similarly, pious Jews would now choose death amid torments rather than agree to break the law (2 Macc. 6:23; 7:1–42). These attitudes derive from a belief in resurrection and retribution after death, or in "eternal life" which is mentioned for the first time in Daniel 12:3 and put into explicit relation to the bodily resurrection at the end of time.

The conception of the person as a unitary being conditions the biblical outlook on human alienation. The alienation itself has two dimensions: physical wretchedness and moral wretchedness. Our modern distinction between physical evil and moral evil was not fully and clearly drawn in the Israelite mind.

But, pessimistic though this vision of the human condition is, we also hear, with increasing clarity, a prophetic message of salvation: We will someday be able to draw near to the God of grace, the God of life. And as our downfall proceeded along two parallel and connected lines—sin and death—so our renewal will have to follow two parallel lines—reconciliation with God and restoration of life.

By the time of Jesus the resurrection of the body had become a dogma of Judaism; only the Saduccees, who were heavily influenced by Greek philosophy, dared deny it. On this point, therefore, Jesus took the side of the Pharisees. Consequently, in the

58517

New Testament the person continues to be regarded as a unitary being. The "salvation" Christ came to bring embraces the whole person; it is not simply a "moral salvation" but a complete liberation that aims effectively at bringing the person to his fullness of possible existence.

Let us begin by considering what the synoptic Gospels have to say. For our purpose it is worth highlighting the connection which is implicitly set up among sin, illness, and the devil. Thus Jesus proclaims the kingdom of God not only by his preaching but also by his action of healing illnesses and casting out demons: "God anointed him with the Holy Spirit and power. He went about doing good works and healing all who were in the grip of the devil" (Acts 10:38).

In the Jewish view (and they were not completely wrong in this) · illness was both a sign and an effect of a certain enslavement to sin and the devil. We see, for example, that the woman with the bad stoop (Luke 13:11) is not regarded as possessed in the strict sense of the term, yet it is said of her that "for eighteen years [she] had been possessed by a spirit which drained her strength" and that she "has been in the bondage of Satan for eighteen years" (13:16).[8]

Jesus often corrects the false ideas entertained by the Jews in this area, but he preserves what was true in them. He says, for example, that the Galileans slain by Pilate were no more sinful than others (Luke 13:1–5). He tells his disciples that the affliction of the man born blind was not due to his own sins or the sins of his parents (John 9:2–3).

Christ gives his disciples the power to heal illnesses and to expel demons (Mark 3:15). The same idea is expressed in positive terms when Jesus is represented as giving or restoring "salvation."

The word "salvation" is used in the synoptic Gospels chiefly in its most basic sense, the common one in classical Greek, in which the verb "to save" was derived from an adjective meaning "sound, entire, healthy."[9] "To save," then, means to restore health to someone who has lost it or security to someone threatened, or to rescue from death someone who is about to perish (cf. Matt. 8:25; 14:30; 27:40, 49; Mark 3:4; Luke 6:9).

In these texts Jesus is usually seen as the author of an immediate, concrete kind of salvation; he "saves" his disciples from the storm and Peter from drowning, but he does not "save" himself from the torment of the cross. The reason for this kind of language is that the New Testament does not think in terms of the salvation of the body, on the one side, and the salvation of the soul, on the other. It thinks simply of the person as unitary.

As Bonnard observes, if Jesus came to "help" the one who is threatened by all sorts of immediate dangers, the help has, in the New Testament view, a special character. It proclaims and makes a reality, in one or other limited sector of human life, a salvation that is definitive and universal in scope; it attests that the time for final salvation has come and that God is now coming to our aid in a way that he has not done up to now (Matt. 11:2–6).[10]

In this respect a great deal of interest attaches to an ambiguous phrase that is frequently found in the synoptic Gospels: "Your faith has saved you" (Mark 5:34; 10:52; Luke 7:50; 8:48; 17:19; 18:42). The context shows that "salvation" refers directly and concretely to the cure that has been effected. Yet a comparison with other strictly parallel texts obliges us not to limit the meaning of "save" to the physical cure alone. In Luke 7:50, for example, the same words are addressed to the public sinner who had wept at the feet of Jesus. The salvation given to this woman was in the area of what we would call the spiritual, the forgiveness of her sins.

It is preferable, therefore, to give the concept of salvation the full scope it clearly has in the synoptic Gospels. The evil from which Jesus comes to free humankind in a definitive way is not sin alone nor physical evil alone, but both, as connected factors in the one catastrophe from which we will be liberated by the saving action of the Messiah.

Death as such is the enemy of God. For God is Life and the Creator of life. It is not by the will of God that there are withering and decay, dying and sickness, the by-products of death working in our life. All these things, according to Christian and Jewish thinking, come from human sin. There-fore, every healing which Jesus accomplishes is not only a driving back of death, but also an invasion of the province of sin; and therefore on every occasion Jesus says: "Your sins are forgiven." Not as though there were a corresponding sin for every individual sickness; but rather, like the presence of death, the fact that sickness exists at all is a consequence of the sinful condition of the whole of humanity. Every healing is a partial resurrection, a partial victory of life over death. That is the Christian point of view. According to the Greek interpretation, on the contrary, bodily sickness is a corollary of the fact that the body is bad in itself and is ordained to destruction. For the Christian an anticipation of the Resurrection can already become visible, even in the earthly body.[11]

In summary: The person whose salvation is proclaimed on every page of the Bible is the person in his entirety, the person as he exists in history. "Salvation" embraces his whole being: moral and physical, soul and body. Later on, we shall see how, according to the Bible, this salvation becomes a reality.

THE PERSON AS NEIGHBOR

As we have just seen, according to the Bible the object of saving love is the whole person, the whole existential reality of the person. But this statement does not exhaust what revealed morality has to say about love.

The person whom the Bible sees as capable of salvation is not the species-being of Marxist anthropology, but the individual in the total concrete context of his inalienable historical existence.

The parable of the Samaritan (Luke 10:29–37) is a joyous poem about the dignity of the human person. Why did the priest and the Levite pass by? Had they not read, day after day, the text from Deuteronomy that the scribe so readily supplied when asked by Jesus: "You shall love your neighbor as yourself"?

Those churchmen had certainly faced the problem of love of neighbor, but they had resolved it at the level of the species and not of the individual. They belonged to a class—the priesthood—which made attention to the neighbor one of its habitual concerns. They themselves probably played an active role in some of the charitable agencies that flourished in the shadow of the temple. But perhaps they had come to think that helping such a poor wounded wretch as this was a waste of time that might be better spent. It might be better spent, for example, in establishing a charitable organization that might put an end to the highway robbers and prevent the roads from being strewn with their victims.

In short, the priest and the Levite believed that their "neighbor" was an institution, not a concrete individual person. They lived in a social climate in which myths—among them, that of the person as a species-being—were substituted for the ever changing realities of the moment.

Today, more than ever, we are facing the problem represented by those poor Israelite victims of misfortune.

The common denominator in the experience of the rising generation is what we might call "the decline of myths." Myths have lost their validity, and young people are now confronting the person as he is: as he sits in his dressing-room, stripped of wig and other stage devices, wearied and sad. The curtain has fallen on the many comedies that used to be played on the stage of our ancient cities; life as it really is has begun. We can no longer approach other people in ready-made roles that are sprinkled with syllogisms and garnished with Latin texts.

No, we must approach them as they really are: small and wretched. As we are, with all our imperfections. We must address them in our own everyday words, and not just in the words of the homily from a pulpit wreathed in incense. We must approach them with a genuinely personal effort, and with our own smile and our own pain; in a word, with an understanding that is really our own. And all this in a completely honest way—no comedy, no stage tricks, no paternalism.

Unfortunately, the New Commandment continues to be something new for many of our own people; the Gospel is still a book with uncut leaves.

The essence of evangelical morality is *love of neighbor:* not just love, but love "of neighbor," of the concrete person beside me. It is easy to love humanity, but it solves no real problems. The priest and the Levite loved humanity; they had their benevolent organizations and thought they had done their whole duty. But they paid no attention to John Henry Smith, forty years old, married, five children, out of work, wearing a week-old beard and a sullen face.

Miguel de Unamuno wrote on our present subject:

Homo sum; nihil humani a me alienum puto [I am a man; nothing human
is foreign to me], said the Latin playwright. And I would rather say,
Nullum hominem a me alienum puto: I am a man; no other man do I
deem a stranger. For to me the adjective *humanus* is no less suspect than
its abstract substantive *humanitas,* humanity. Neither "the human" nor
"humanity," neither the simple adjective nor the substantivized adjective, but the concrete substantive—man. The man of flesh and bone; the
man who is born, suffers, and dies—above all, who dies; the man who
eats and drinks and plays and sleeps and thinks and wills; the man who is
seen and heard; the brother, the real brother.[12]

Gabriel Marcel says that genuine love reaches out to the person
insofar as he is not categorizable, to the concrete person whose
situation cannot be classified in any of the countless pigeonholes
set up by even the most complex welfare state.

Love of neighbor—of this particular neighbor who is next to
me—requires a great capacity for improvisation and a ceaseless
effort to overcome the relentless tyranny of the filing system. In his
impressive novel, *The Twenty-Fifth Hour*, Gheorghiu has shown
us how powerful a bureaucracy can be in its blind threat to crush
the vital spontaneity of age-old human communities.

True love of neighbor can never be kept within the metal prison
of a faultless filing system.

The attitude of improvisation required by Christian love for the
concrete individual person supposes a great respect for individual
liberty. The person must freely shape his own existence; he must
make decisions that determine his own life. This does not mean, of
course, that we must leave him isolated in Rousseau's forest where
he may attempt the impossible task of forming himself without
help from anyone else.

No, we need collaborators, but we do not need people to
suppress our freedom. To educate another is an immensely difficult task, and the educator may readily yield to the temptation of
using desperate remedies and of banging the table in order to
produce a seeming order and give the impression that here
"human beings are being formed."

But the impression is only a mirage. Many mass-people are
victims of such a throttling of freedom, and once they are out on
their own, they react in ways determined by what they inwardly

admire but with which they are not yet totally in harmony. In the ambience created by these masses there sometimes spring up, like exotic plants, individuals endowed with penetrating powers of reflection and a strong tendency to affirm their own freedom in an honorable way.

Their attitude brings no little trouble upon them. Inevitably they try to construct a theory that will account for each small step taken in real life. Everything is subjected to a rigid control by reflection, the kind of reflection that moves from premise to premise until the poor dialectical pilgrim is wearied and discouraged.

At this point the thinker is often tempted to jettison everything and to be as others: those who do not think, those who improvise from moment to moment, those who do not ask why and wherefore. He sees other people happy, self-assured, victorious over life, and he fears that his own outlook may be quixotic, absurd, and thoroughly impracticable. Yet he cannot bring himself to adopt that other manner of life; he is like David when he donned Saul's armor: He cannot walk in it. Then, inevitably, he turns back to his thinking and each time finds it more convincing, clearer, and more penetrating. But the anxiety does not therefore disappear, for his life is wrenched by a twofold tension.

One of the causes of his anxiety is that he believes himself to be a coldly calculating, heartless individual. The society in which he was born has set up a divorce between "thought" and "action." The poor intellectual is allowed to be an intellectual provided he be a chemically pure one, a Byzantine type who stays shut up in his impenetrable tower and exercises no influence on life and events. Those who control society will not bother him if he remains the pure intellectual; on the contrary, they will boast of him and show him off to foreigners as something unusual and highly decorative.

In a word, society has in this case attempted to substitute standardization for education. This amounts to denying the great mystery of God's presence in the world, namely, his ineffable respect for the person's use of his own freedom. God, the great Educator, leaves the person free and permits him to destroy himself through sin.

Our determination to keep hands off our "neighbor" and to take refuge in "the person as species-being" often springs from a fear of freedom. The "neighbor" is an individual, a concrete being who is unique because he is free. To love this neighbor is to love a free person who, precisely because he is free, demands continual improvisation on our part and exposes us to the danger of failure and rejection.

For this reason, we renounce love of neighbor and take refuge in a pseudolove of humankind. We do not accept the person as he is; we idealize him, we subject him to a process of purification which eliminates the disquieting element that might disturb the peace emanating from the resultant heroic figure we are so proud to exhibit.

In short, we lack love, true Christian love, because we are afraid of our neighbor.

People who, chronologically speaking, have reached a certain maturity begin to feel the itch of responsibility for the maturation of those who come after them. This is the moment when they must be prepared not to fall into the harmful fear of people, of which we have been speaking. For we would like the projected person whose destiny lies in our hands to follow a carefully drawn up pattern. We want our technological workshops to produce copies that imitate in every detail the ideal type we have conceived in our minds.

Here we have the reason why educators so often get annoyed when they cannot explain the bottomless mystery of human freedom. They are afraid of the human person, of his spontaneous reactions, of his weaknesses and limitations. To avoid being surprised by him they have recourse to an essentially antipedagogical method: They enclose him in a sterilized bell jar and cut off his communications with an outside world that might provoke unpleasant reactions from him.

In this way these false pilots of voyaging humankind are enabled to keep a ship's log that shows no surprises: "Nothing new." And with a sense of proud satisfaction they reach port on the shores of life, and deliver their precious human cargo, stamped with the prudent warning: "Very fragile."

It hardly needs saying that this fragile human merchandise will smash itself to pieces as soon as the pitiless longshoremen strip it of its wrappings—the wrappings put on the goods with so much fuss and care by a few dangerous people who did not know how to love their neighbor because they feared the mystery of freedom.

The only Man who could truly call himself Teacher of others was not afraid of freedom, and, as champion of the cause, could forthrightly tell his disciples: "You will suffer in the world. But take courage! I have overcome the world" (John 16:33).

In the gigantic struggle in which our contemporaries are making every effort to monopolize the privilege of forming the "new person" of the immediate future, we Christians cannot forget that the decisive point on which we differ from others is precisely our attitude of love for neighbor, for the concrete, individual person, with all his unforeseeable spontaneities of freedom.

We must also be big enough to acknowledge that our agencies for assistance, our charitable organizations, and our undertakings for rebuilding the social order have been infected with collectivism. They have done what they could to repeat the sad spectacle of "priests" and "levites" who are satisfied with a pseudolove of the person as a species-being and pass by the concrete person who makes himself a bothersome stumbling block on their carefully planned route.

NOTES

1. Cf. Edmond Jacob, *Theology of the Old Testament,* trans. Arthur W. Heathcote and Philip J. Allcock (New York: Harper & Row, 1958), p. 158.

2. Cf. Gen. 6:3; Isa. 31:3; 40:6; 49:26; Jer. 12:12; 17:5; 25:31; 32:27; 45:5; Ezek. 21:4; Ps. 56:5; 65:3; 78:39; 145:21; 2 Chron. 32:8.

3. Cf. Jacob, *Theology of the Old Testament,* p. 312.

4. Ibid.

5. Cf. Adolf Lods, "Le sort des incirconcis," *Comptes rendus de l'Académie des Inscriptions et Belles-Lettres* (1943), p. 271.

6. Jacob, *Theology of the Old Testament,* p. 307.

7. Robert Martin-Achard, *From Death to Life: A Study of the Development of the Doctrine of the Resurrection in the Old Testament,* trans. John Peney Smith (Edinburgh: Oliver and Boyd, 1960), pp. 19–20.

8. Cf. Stanislas Lyonnet, *Theologia Biblica Novi Testamenti* (Rome: Pontifical Biblical Institute, 1956), 1:88.

9. Cf. Pierre Bonnard, *Vocabulario bíblico* (Madrid: Marova, 1968), p. 310.

10. Ibid.

11. Cullmann, *Immortality or Resurrection,* p. 29.

12. Miguel de Unamuno, *Tragic Sense of Life,* trans. J.E. Crawford Flitch (1921; New York: Dover, 1954), p. 1.

CHAPTER 7

THE MORALITY OF LOVE: RESPONSIBLE FOR THE COURSE OF HISTORY

Contemporary Christianity suffers from a serious defect: It has turned its back on the eschatological hope.

For many Christians Christ is identified with the splendid images created by a Martínez Montañés or a Pedro de Mena. They do not adore such images in an idolatrous spirit, but they do regard them as fine portraits of the person who came and gave us an example of how to live.

Furthermore, they believe that Christ lives on and they direct their prayers to him. But in their view Christ has already come, and his work is already completely accomplished. Our task is simply to follow his example and teaching. The ideal is to live a "Christian" life, so that after death we may obtain the final reward that is independent of and has nothing to do with the body, for the body is simply carrion that corrupts and disappears in the grave.

In such a view the return of Christ is for practical purposes eliminated from the horizon of the Christian's real life. Christ has already come. His work is restricted to the limits of our earthly life, and earthly life is regarded as being simply a period of training and preparation for our true life, the life of the separated soul.

These Christians do not long for Christ's return. They are content with his coming on earth. They have already anticipated the glorious manifestation of humankind and reduced it within the narrow limits of space and time.

Christian life is thus identified with an esthetic moralism that stands in hopeless contrast with the terrible tragedy in which humankind is involved. It is a morality that teaches contempt for the body and for human work. Our contemporaries see Christians as cowards who try to escape the catastrophe by taking refuge in an imaginary fortified tower where they foster the deadly illusion that they will find salvation in a world created by their own imaginings.

St. Paul saw that such an outlook was possible, and he drew back in horror from the possibility. If Christianity meant only a fine moral life that unfolded exclusively within the limits of our present existence with all its defects, then it would not be worth the effort of adhering to Christianity.

BIOLOGICAL POWER OF LOVE FOR NEIGHBOR

Using a comparison derived from Greco-Roman law, Paul says that the Christian is like a son who passes from the status of a slave to a genuinely filial relationship with his father. But he makes it clear that even this new situation is not the final and definitive one. The reason is that the son can now make free use of his father's possessions, but he has still to enter into his inheritance. The Christian, therefore, is already a son of God, but he is also an heir; Christians are "the heirs he [Abraham] was promised" (Gal. 3:29 JB), the Christian is "an heir, by God's design" (Gal. 4:7).

The term "to inherit" (*kleronomein*) referred in the Old Testament to the promise God had made to Israel that it would some day take possession of the land of Canaan. One who is an heir does not yet possess the reality, although he does have the root of it. Nonetheless, the Old Testament usually speaks of giving, at some unfixed future date, the *kleronomia* of the promised land (Gen. 15:7; Deut. 30:5; Num. 34:2; etc.). Consequently, the verb *kleronomein* (to inherit) can also mean to take possession of the land.

This *kleronomia,* or inheritance, founded a permanent right of possession. This is why in jubilee years the land had to pass back into the effective possession of its first masters. It is also why the concept of *kleronomia* could be transferred to the eschatological sphere, since it was especially apt for expressing the eternal possession of the kingdom of God.

The term begins to be used in this eschatological sense in the New Testament. Thus, the lowly "shall inherit the land" (Matt. 5:5). The rich young man asks: "What must I do to share in ['to inherit'] everlasting life?" (Mark 10:17). Paul says that "flesh and blood cannot inherit the kingdom of God" (1 Cor. 15:50). This entering into possession of the kingdom of God is identified with the eschatological resurrection of the body, of which chapter 15 is speaking. Consequently, being an heir supposes the present possession of the Spirit and the possibility and guarantee of the future resurrection.

The doctrine of the resurrection thus proves to be the cornerstone in the structure of the Apostle's religious thought. His Christology, his soteriology, and his anthropology all have it as their center.

We can distinguish two points in Paul's teaching on the resurrection:

1. The affirmation of Christian hope in the resurrection. That hope could not be uprooted from hearts whose sensibility had been formed by reading the Old Testament. For, though the Old Testament says little about resurrection, it differs from most Greek and Eastern religions in teaching that the creation of the visible world and the human body is not a deplorable accident that was brought about by the fall of spirits, but a manifestation of divine wisdom that is not lessened by the later fall. An eschatology, therefore, that teaches that the world will simply be destroyed, and is content with hoping for the heavenly immortality of the soul alone, cannot do justice to creation as understood by the Old Testament. What a Christian wants is "a new heaven and a new earth," that is, a new creation.

2. The affirmation that this hope will be fulfilled. On what is this certainty based? The Apostle might have been satisfied to refer to a revelation on this point, as he was in the First Epistle to the Thessalonians. But he wants to go further and connect it with a definitive fact that is attested by witnesses (1 Cor. 15:1–11).

After adducing the fact, Paul uses an argument based on absurd consequences. The Corinthians were denying the resurrection of the dead, for they were heavily influenced by Greek philosophy, which scorned the body and maintained that the spirit alone was essential. But then the Corinthians must deny the resurrection of Christ as well. But that was, logically, an absurd position for Christians whose faith had for its very object the resurrection of Christ (1 Cor. 15:12–13). For it follows that the whole of apostolic preaching, which has its main basis in the great witness of Christ's resurrection, will be entirely lacking in foundation, and that therefore the very faith of the Corinthians will be emptied of its content. The consequences would be disastrous:

1. Faith would be a worthless illusion (*mataia*), a myth, a social fiction; it would not be based on a real historical fact.

2. The first step in the overall process of redemption would not have been taken, namely, liberation from sin—"You are still in your sins" (1 Cor. 15:17). Moreover, for Paul sin and death form but a single portion as do reconciliation and resurrection; therefore sin is not overcome in isolation, but death is also conquered with it. If, then, Christ has not risen, death has not been overcome any more than sin has.

3. The Christian dead are lost; they have fallen into "eternal" death, or death that knows no hope of resurrection.

In brief, "if our hopes in Christ are limited to this life only, we are the most pitiable of men" (1 Cor. 15:19). For Paul, as for all the biblical writers, the survival of the separated soul is not in the proper sense "life." Life is something integral and inclusive, and requires embodiment. Consequently, if Christianity meant only a refined moral life aimed solely at regulating human actions within the narrow framework of our present life and brought with it no sure hope of regaining life beyond death, it would not be worth bothering about.

Pauline morality is wholly focused on expectation and hope. The expectation will not be fulfilled by adopting a merely passive attitude, a kind of relaxation of soul in the face of a future breakthrough of the divine; on the contrary, expectation and its fulfillment imply a constant activity, a continuous effort to overcome the "tendencies" of the flesh. Only thus can we understand the emphasis with which Paul exhorts the faithful to form their lives according to new principles.

He sees a radical opposition between two moral attitudes which he calls flesh and spirit. "Those who live according to the flesh are intent on the things of the flesh, those who live according to the spirit, on those of the spirit. The tendency [*phronema*: aim, aspiration, striving] of the flesh is toward death but that of the spirit toward life and peace" (Rom. 8:5–6).

The "life" toward which moral conduct "in the spirit" tends is precisely the life that is wholly regained through resurrection. Therefore, as long as Christ dwells in Christians through the Spirit, it does not matter that sin still sinks its claws into them by making them die, for "the spirit lives because of justice" (Rom. 8:10). That is, the justified person has within himself the hope and pledge of life: "If the Spirit of him who raised Jesus from the dead dwells in you, then he who raised Jesus from the dead will bring your mortal bodies to life also through his Spirit dwelling in you" (Rom. 8:11).

Christian morality thus goes beyond the limits of pure ethics and lays hold on the person's very biology. By this I mean that the person of the Spirit does not simply build up his "moral life"; he builds a life that is complete and all-embracing. "If you live according to the flesh, you will die; but if by the spirit you put to death the evil deeds of the body, you will live" (Rom. 8:13).

But the Christian is also existentially rooted and planted in the world, in the totality or "fulness" of creation. Paul tells us that his thoughts on this point have been carefully weighed and are the fruit of reflection (*logizomai*: "I consider . . . "—Rom. 8:18).

Suffering in fellowship with Christ is framed in a much wider context. It must be considered in its integral connection with future glory. The present and the visible can be understood only in the light of the future and invisible, i.e. in the light of that new world and aeon which God has begun to establish with the coming of Christ and whose action, secret but certain, is rendered already effective through communion with Christ in the Holy Spirit. . . .

Because we live in the flesh, we still share in the general destinies of the world. Our state of suffering has something in common with the suffering of the world; our personal situation compels us to think about that of creation as a whole. Now the whole of creation aspires towards the fulfillment of the ends which God has assigned to it. Its situation is a historical one; it is engaged in a process of movement; it waits expectantly. The advent of Christ gives a new justification to its expectancy. For in Him creation can recover the orientation towards its original destiny of which it has been frustrated by the disobedience of man. Christ institutes at the heart of creation the new humanity of the "children of God." Through Him, man, restored to his filial relation with God, will be able to subject creation to that useful work which was its original purpose; and thus he will serve creation by mastering it. In this way he will reveal himself to it as the bearer of the image of God placed at the summit of the creative process, to exercise there, according to the will of God, his beneficent authority; he will be disclosed universally as the new man for whom creation is longing that it may attain its goal.[1]

In light of this we can easily understand the exhortation with which Paul ends his explanation of morality to the Galatians: "Make no mistake about it, no one makes a fool of God! A man will reap only what he sows. If he sows in the field of the flesh, he will reap a harvest of corruption; but if his seed-ground is the spirit, he will reap everlasting life" (Gal. 6:7–8).

The image of sowing and reaping was well known in Greco-Roman moral philosophy, but it was also current in the Old Testament. In its biblical context, the point of the image is not precisely the natural correspondence between moral acts and their "purely moral" consequences, but rather the relation between moral conduct and God's judgment (cf. Hos. 8:7; Prov. 22:8; Joel 3:13; cf. also Luke 19:21; 1 Cor. 9:11; etc.).

Paul speaks here of "corruption" (phthora) as the eschatological destiny of the person-as-flesh. We have the same expression and context as in 1 Corinthians 15:50–54, where "corruption" refers to death and is contrasted with the eschatological resurrection (aphtharsia, "incorruption").

Christian morality has its place within historical human evolution, where its function is not to be simply a rule of conduct but to be a biological seed of fulfillment. Christianity's answer to the human question: "How is the person to form himself?" is simply this: Through incorporation into Christ the person enters into possession of the divine Spirit, who enables him to put into effect a plan of "justice" that not only improves him but puts him effectively on the road to the fulfillment of humankind's age-old dream: the definitive conquest of death.

The whole of creation anxiously waits for us Christians to bring fully into effective operation the law of brotherly love. For that law will not only make better human beings; it will also hasten the process of humankind's biological and existential maturation.

Our indolence when it comes to love is a crime against history, for we are responsible for the prolongation of the human tragedy and for the fact that the day of complete human liberation will not dawn soon.

CHRISTIANS: RESPONSIBLE FOR HISTORY

The idea of biological maturation which is inherent in Christian morality is not something peripheral or accidental in the Bible. On the contrary, it is necessary for a proper understanding of the revealed message itself.

I shall limit myself here to the outlook of Paul, especially in his use of the historico-progressive conception as the supreme motivation in Christian ethics and mysticism. The whole of his thought is dominated by the idea, and consequently we can see this ''theology of history'' at work from his earliest writings down to the works of his maturity.

FIRST EPISTLE TO THE CORINTHIANS

Divine wisdom and the foolishness of the Cross (1 Cor. 1:17–2:5)

The Corinthians are divided by considerations based on human wisdom. But the good news of salvation is the proclamation of the cross of Christ, which is a stumbling block to the Jews and foolishness to the Greeks—those decadent Greeks who have departed from their great teachers and gotten lost in the maze of convoluted argumentation. Paul is not defending ignorance. The Greeks have, in fact, worked out a correct ethics and an acceptable theodicy; but their practice lags far behind their principles, and therefore God falls back on paradox; he chooses the ignorant and the weak to confound the strong.

Paul, then, is rejecting pagan wisdom, not insofar as it contains elements of wisdom, but insofar as it does not correspond to the plan of God for the world.

Almost all the philosophies of antiquity—Indian or Persian, Greek or Latin—seem to agree on one doctrine: the world is eternal. Since, however, the world is not changeless, it passes through the same states from time to time. Thus the heaven, made up of incorruptible bodies, periodically passes through the same conflagration; the world of corruptible things experiences alternating floods and fires which determine its rhythm and mark the periodic return of the same kinds of things. Only Christian philosophy will reject this thesis that the universe is eternal and marked by periodicity.[2]

Christian wisdom (1 Cor. 2:6–16)

Over against the pagan outlook on the world and the person stands a revealed wisdom that the Spirit has made known to the elect. Paul speaks of it as a wisdom for the spiritually mature (*teleioi*). The content of this wisdom is God's plan for the world: The rulers of this ''age'' (this historical situation) are headed for destruction; in other words, the present age is wounded mortally, and the thorn of the future age is buried deep within its very bosom. Such is the ''wisdom of God in mystery'' which God has prepared before the ages for our glory. Here, then, is a vision of history that embraces both world and person; it is now in process of fulfillment, and at the end of it is our glory. The glory of the human person is not independent of matter but rather means the fulfillment of matter, as Paul will later explain in chapter 15 when he deals with the eschatological resurrection.

Humankind's task in the building of history (1 Cor. 3:1–23)

The Corinthians are still people of flesh and ''children'' in Christ, immature Christians; they do not yet understand this ''wisdom'' or plan of God. They do not know that all are called to build the great temple of God, the eschatological temple of his final kingdom.

Paul mixes two metaphors, building and sowing. He is dealing with history, and the Apostles are simply workmen on the building, farmlaborers tending God's plants in history. There is no question here of human philosophies invented by the wise; there is no point to making Paul or Apollos the focal point in the Christian rhythm of history. God is the one who causes the growth.

Christians, and especially the Apostles, are the hired co-workers of God; under God, they have responsibility for the progressive building of history. The "Day of the Lord," that is, of divine eschatological judgment, will make known what each worker has contributed to the construction of the whole building.

That judgment will be like a fire; the more solid the material used, the more it will resist the fire. There will be cases where the material is only straw and cannot resist the testing by fire; the work done by any given worker may be objectively without value, yet the worker himself can be saved like a person fleeing with great difficulty through the fire, saving himself but none of his possessions. In brief, the kingdom of God is built gradually; the toil of the evangelical workers not only yields merits to be rewarded in the next life, but also contributes objectively to the progressive development of history in the direction of Christ, until it reaches the final stage of *anakephalaiosis* or "recapitulation" in Christ (Eph. 1:10).

Paul ends this section of his letter by exhorting the Corinthians not to let themselves be led astray by other conceptions of the world and the person. The Christian has full responsibility for the course of history: "All things are yours, whether it be Paul, or Apollos, or Cephas, or the world, or life, or death, or the present, or the future: all these are yours." True, provided one indispensable condition is met—that "you are Christ's"; that is, that Christians act in the name of Christ, who is the key to the world and to history (1 Cor. 3:22–23).

Christianity, then, is a "philosophy" that does not set out simply to offer a speculative explanation of the world and the person, but aims essentially at improving them and bringing them to their definitive maturity.

In chapter 15 Paul will speak clearly and explicitly of the goal of this Christian development of history to its maturity: the resurrection of humankind and the inauguration of God's kingdom. In the present chapter we have the great charter for the theology of history in the fact that Christianity looks with high seriousness on human effort expended according to "the mind of Christ," as an essentially constructive factor in achieving the definitive goal of humankind.

*The kingdom of God has not yet come but is still coming
(1 Cor. 4:1–21)*

The outlook of the Corinthians is lacking in historical perspective, for they have arrogated to themselves nothing less than the right to "judge," an action which cannot be carried out "before the time of his return" (1 Cor. 4:5). Even the Apostles, for all their indisputable authority, are only "administrators of the mysteries of God" (4:1). That is, they carry out, within time, those hidden plans of God for the glorious development and maturation of the world in Christ.

The Corinthians think they have already reached the kingdom. Paul addresses them in ironic tones: "At the moment you are completely satisfied. You have grown rich! You have launched upon your reign with no help from us" (1 Cor. 4:8). How odd, he continues, that it should be the Corinthians, and not the Apostles, who have lightheartedly reached the kingdom, as they see the situation! Certainly, the Apostles are not yet there! "God has put us Apostles at the end of the line, like men doomed to die in the arena. We have become a spectacle to the universe, to angels and men alike" (1 Cor. 4:9). They have become the world's refuse (*perikathermata*); the reference is not simply to expendable people generally but to ones who, in a rite known in Asia Minor, were sacrificed to the gods in order to win relief from certain calamities; since the sacrifice was voluntary, only the most unfortunate of beggars offered themselves as victims, for the reason that they would be well treated until the time for the sacrifice.

More than once in its history Christianity has known the temptation to which the community at Corinth succumbed: that of thinking itself rich, of being satisfied with what had hitherto been accomplished, and of mistaking a temporary encampment for the "lasting city," towards which history is moving under the guidance of the Church.

Sexuality and the resurrection (1 Cor. 6:12–20)

Paul introduces into the area of sexual morality an extrinsic motivation of which the Greek world had known nothing: "The body is not for immorality; it is for the Lord, and the Lord is for the body. God, who raised up the Lord, will raise us also by his power" (1 Cor. 6:13–14).

To understand this passage, we must suppose the existence at Corinth of a group of libertine gnostics, similar to those whom later antiheretical polemicists would be fighting (Clement of Alexandria, Irenaeus, and others). The doctrine of this group had two basic principles: (1) The life of the body and all that is concerned with it is of no significance for the spiritual life and destiny of the soul. Therefore, carnal excesses cannot stain the spirit, which alone inherits the kingdom of God. (2) The body, like all other material things, was created by an inferior divinity. Consequently, there is no bodily resurrection.

The second principle was common to all gnostics; the first was peculiar to those who accepted libertinism. The latter was opposed by those gnostics who were inclined toward asceticism and strove to mortify the flesh in order to liberate the spirit; sometimes they forbade marriage (cf. 1 Cor. 7; 1 Tim. 4:3). The people with whom Paul is in conflict professed both of the basic principles mentioned: libertinism (1 Cor. 6, 8) and denial of the resurrection (1 Cor. 15).

The Apostle's counterattack is inspired by two considerations:

1. *The biblical teaching on the creation of the body.* According to the Bible, God created not only souls and spirits but bodies as well and, in a general way, all material things. Material creation was, admittedly, perverted by the Fall. The body became "fleshly." But to be material is not necessarily to be "fleshly," and the body, as a material being, has its proper place in creation. For this reason it too will enter the kingdom of heaven as a body freed from corruption and fulfilling the ideal of purified materiality that is at the service of the Holy Spirit. This is why every sin against the body is also a sin against the will of God and may prevent a person from inheriting the kingdom.

2. *The Christian conception of the Eucharist.* The general consideration based on creation is reinforced by a specific consideration proper to Christians: their membership in the body of Christ. This membership is not purely spiritual or mystical; it is also material and quasiphysical. The body of Christ, in the Apostle's

view, is a metahistorical reality which, thanks to the Eucharist (1 Cor. 11), extends its dominion into the historical sphere where the future resurrectional body is being prepared. Conduct, therefore, which loses sight of the body's noble destiny can undermine the action of the Spirit and our belonging to Christ.

Paul thus offers his readers a very high kind of motive: "You must know that your body is a temple of the Holy Spirit, who is within—the Spirit you have received from God" (1 Cor. 6:19). The image of the temple of the Spirit had already been used in 3:16, but there it was applied to the Church as a whole. Here it is the individual human body that is to become a dwelling for the Spirit. This ideal will be realized in a visible way only in the future age, in the world of resurrection. But the Holy Spirit must here and now take possession of the Christian person and prepare him for his future state.

Sacramental liturgy and the salvational rhythm of history (1 Cor. 11:17–34)

The faithful used to gather in "assemblies" (*ekklesiai*) in order to celebrate the rite of the Eucharistic Supper. These gatherings, however, were going from bad to worse (1 Cor. 11:17). What Paul is blaming the Corinthians for is the lack of love and community that marked some of these Eucharistic gatherings, where there were divisions (*schismata*) and factions (*haireseis*) such as militated against the very nature of a community gathering. But there is no evil from which some good may not result, and the evils now afflicting the community bring to light the true quality of the Christians who make it up.

When the Corinthians gather as they do, it cannot be said that what they celebrate is really "the Lord's Supper," "for everyone is in haste to eat his own supper" (1 Cor. 11:21). Instead of waiting until all have assembled and the food that various members have brought has been equitably distributed, the rich quickly eat what they have without waiting for the others—the poor—who, of course, have had to spend a longer time at their work. A further abuse is that the rich overeat and overdrink. Now, such abuses are manifestations of contempt for "the church [assembly] of God," precisely because they "embarrass those who have nothing" (1 Cor. 11:22). It is clear from what Paul says that in the church of God at Corinth the poor were regarded as inferior.

As a basis for his exhortation Paul harkens back to his catechesis on the Eucharist and then says: "Every time, then, you eat this bread and drink this cup, you proclaim the death of the Lord until he comes!" (1 Cor. 11:26). The Eucharistic rite is a proclamation of the Lord's death. Throughout Paul's theology the present state of the Christian is described as an "incorporation into the death of the Lord" (cf. Rom. 6:2–11). But Christ's death is not an end point, but a passage to resurrection and life (ibid.). In fact, the extension of the Lord's death to us brings salvation, because this death is one that is immediately overcome in resurrection. Nonetheless, "until the Lord comes," our resurrection is real only in the order of promise.

The Church is responsible for seeing to it that the saving efficacy of Christ's death is progressively extended to all people. The Eucharistic sacrifice makes the death of Christ present, so that every time the Mass is celebrated the distance between death and resurrection is shortened. The sacrifice of the individual Christ, of Christ who was the first fruits, was a passage from death to life. Humankind as a whole is now slowly making the same passage. First it is incorporated through baptism into the death of Christ; then it gradually works its way through a series of stages, especially with the help of the celebration or "proclamation" of Christ's death in the Eucharistic rite.

Paul goes on to tell his Corinthian readers that to eat the body of the Lord and drink his blood unworthily, as they do when they fail so seriously in brotherly love, is really to attempt in a sacrilegious way to destroy the saving efficacy of Christ's death; it is to "sin against the body and blood of the Lord." Such sinful doings act as a kind of brake to slow down the movement toward the Parousia which the Eucharistic sacrifice would, of itself, speed up. The Corinthians are trying, as it were, to "kill" Christ again and to render his death ineffective (cf. Heb. 6:6; 10:29).

In the Corinthian community "many . . . are sick and infirm, and . . . many are dying" (1 Cor. 11:30). In this state of affairs Paul sees a divine punishment. As long as the Christian community does not fulfill its task of hastening the Parousia (in this instance, by correctly celebrating the Eucharist), then the basic human ills—suffering and death—will continue to afflict it. When Christians do not live up to their constructive task in relation to the Parousia, they are responsible for prolonging the tragedy of humankind.

It is undoubtedly true that the sacramental presence of Christ within human history is effecting, from within, its biological maturation toward the existential fulfillment of the resurrection. But sacramental action requires human cooperation. The movement toward the Parousia which is inherent in "the proclamation of the Lord's death" in the Eucharistic rite can be brutally checked, if the Eucharist is not celebrated by a genuinely Christian gathering that is wholly permeated by brotherly love.

The point of convergence: Parousia, resurrection, and inauguration of metahistory (1 Cor. 15)

Paul begins this chapter with a solemn reminder of the gospel he had preached at Corinth. He had preached the basic fact—Christ's resurrection—without which the faith of the Corinthians would be an empty thing, a blind belief lacking in any deep conviction and therefore unable to rescue them from the doubt and despair which sooner or later would attack them (1 Cor. 15:1–2). He will examine this fundamental fact of Christian belief in this part of his letter.

After experiencing a certain anxiety simply from imagining the possibility of there being no resurrection, Paul breathes easily again as he acknowledges anew the tangible reality of the concrete, material, thoroughly verifiable fact of Christ's resurrection: "But as it is, Christ is now raised from the dead, the first fruits of those who have fallen asleep" (1 Cor. 15:20). Christ's resurrection is a real fact with both individual and collective significance: He himself has passed out of the realm of the dead and he has also opened the door so that those who cleave to him may likewise pass through it. "Those who have fallen asleep" (ibid.) accurately describes those who "die in Christ," for their death is a purely temporary state.

Christ is the second Adam. Adam compelled *his* human race to die; Christ will bring those who belong to him to resurrection (1 Cor. 15:20–22).

There is, however, a hierarchy in time: Christ is already risen, as the first being of the new world; later, "at his coming, all those who belong to him" will also rise (1 Cor. 15:23) and, with this event, the *present* history of humankind will be at its end. Paul imagines this ending taking place as follows: Christ, as commander-in-chief of the army of liberation that has fought throughout history for the kingdom of God, will hand over the fruits of his conquest to the Father, for all enemies have now been overcome (verse 24). The final enemy to be destroyed is death (verse 26); this conception of death as the final enemy is, as we have seen, radically opposed to the Socratic and Platonic view of death as the great friend who frees the person from what is not truly himself: the body or antiperson. As a result of this ending of the long struggle, God will be "all in all" (verse 28). Paul is speaking here not of a pantheism (everything absorbed into God) but of a panentheism (God completely present everywhere through the perfect exercise of his rule).

Paul now goes on to offer some secondary proofs, derived from the persuasion of the faithful and from his own persuasion, inasmuch as Christian conduct is commanded by the goal of resurrection. Verses 30–31 are fairly clear: If there were no resurrection, the dangerous life of an apostle would not be worth living. He had been obliged, at Ephesus (whence he was writing his letter to the Corinthians) to fight with beasts (thus anticipating the later martyrs). If he had done so "for purely human motives," without any hope of resurrection, what would have been the point of it all? If the dead do not rise, then the Epicureans are right: "Let us eat and drink, for tomorrow we die!" (verse 32).

Paul ends this part of the chapter with an exhortation to be on guard against a serious danger: "Do not be led astray any longer. 'Bad company corrupts good morals' " (1 Cor. 15:33). Here he is quoting a proverb from the writings of the poet Menander; those who were denying the resurrection were close to falling into libertinism. Without keeping the resurrection in view, a person cannot live a serious life; in other words, deny the resurrection and you may end up "ignorant of God" (verse 34), lacking in genuine "knowledge" of God. And that would be a truly shameful state. In brief: Paul cannot conceive of a Christian moral life that is not inspired by hope of the resurrection.

How will the resurrection take place? Paul uses an example from the plant world, although he is laying no claim to accurate knowledge of plant biology. To the onlooker, the grain of wheat seems to die when it is sown, and to rise again as transformed into the luxuriant ear. Of course, God's power intervenes in the process. But we must observe that each kind of seed yields a specific kind of body (human beings, animals, birds, fish). So it is with the resurrection: Every seed that "dies" in the furrow yields a particular glorified body.

The risen body will be *the same in identity* as the mortal body, but *not the same in quality,* for the corruptible will become incorruptible, the ignoble glorious, the weak strong: In other words: A "natural" *(physikon)* body is sown, and a "spiritual" *(pneumatikon)* body rises up.

The allusion to the natural and spiritual bodies allows Paul to treat the narrative of Genesis in a Midrashic way. According to Gen. 2:7 the first Adam became a "living soul" *(psyche zosa),* that is, simply a natural bodily being. But the second Adam is a "life-giving spirit" *(pneuma zoopoioun),* a supernatural being who gives life to others. This latter gathers all humankind about himself in order to bring it with him to heaven. If, then, we want to reach resurrection, we must leave the first Adam's sphere of influence and be incorporated into Christ.

Paul ends the chapter with a brief exposition of the "mystery" (1 Cor. 15:51) of which he had earlier spoken in writing to the Thessalonians (cf. 1 Thess. 4:15–17). This mystery is that, at the moment of Christ's coming, those still alive on earth will not die but will be changed by being given glorified bodies. At this moment humankind's corruptible existence will be ended, and its final, lasting period will begin.

The practical conclusion: "Be steadfast and persevering, my beloved brothers, fully engaged in the work of the Lord. You know that your toil is not in vain when it is done in the Lord" (1 Cor. 15:58).

Evidently, faith in the resurrection is absolutely essential in Paul's eyes and provides the chief moral motive for the work a Christian does. Christians toil for themselves and others with a very concrete end in view: the progressive formation of a race that will someday reach the perfect maturity of the resurrection. The hope with which the Christian toils is not purely passive, as though the resurrection were to come ready-made out of heaven. Rather, he truly acts and has an effect on human relationships and sows in them the seed of resurrection.

EPISTLE TO THE ROMANS

The message of the Epistle to the Romans is valid for all times and places and can be understood only in the light of the preoccupation with history that is so central to Pauline soteriology.

Paul contemplated the deed wrought by Christ and was forced to ask what meaning it had for human relationships. What was the state of humankind before his coming? What is humankind's state without Christ? What has Christ done for humankind? What kind of liberation, healing, elevation, and salvation has he effected?

Before Christ and apart from Christ people have looked for answers to the problem of salvation for the individual and for society. Paul divides humankind into two large groups: pagans and Jews.

The pagans (Rom. 1:18–32) had the help of natural reason and even succeeded in developing a noble philosophy, with an acceptable ethics and an accurate theodicy. Despite all this, the pagan world was a desolating sight. People were still filled with anxiety and plunging ever deeper into the mire of a terrible moral degradation.

The Jews (Rom. 2:3–8) possessed a special divine revelation and a social structure that was imposed by God himself; these were both manifested in the Law. But for all that the human situation in Jewish society was not much more attractive than in paganism. Israel experienced no less anxiety and despair in the face of the human problem than did the Greco-Roman world.

Paul then tries to highlight as best he can the universal significance of Christ as the total and definitive answer to the human problem. The exposition of this answer takes up the first eight chapters of the Epistle.

The liberating action of Christ moves through two stages: first, liberation from sin, then the definitive conquest of death. In daily life the Christian seems to be simply a person-in-Adam; like the person in Adam, he too dies. But there is in fact a great difference, for the Christian dies in Christ, since in baptism he has been incorporated into the death of Christ. This means that the Christian's death is not the end of the line but a time of waiting; it is not a final destruction but a sowing of the seed of resurrection (Rom. 6:3–4). The Christian, like the pagan, dies, but his death is only a sleep. For to die in Christ means to die the same death that Christ died; in other words, the Christian dies a death from which there is an escape, a death from which he shall some day rise to life in the resurrection.

The connection between the historical situation of reconciliation and the future state of resurrection is not formed simply by the bridge of hope. To be a Christian is not simply a matter of nourishing within one's heart the hope of the great day of resurrection. No, the Christian must help bring to maturity within this world the seed of that life and happiness which are the definitive goal of history; "All creation groans and is in agony even until now," as it "eagerly awaits the revelation of the sons of God" (Rom. 8:22, 19).

We Christians are called upon to shape the world. We are responsible for the world moving toward Christ, as it must if human history is ever to enter upon its golden age. If we do not exercise toward creation the ministry we have received in regard to it, then creation will not be mastered and will not advance toward the end assigned to it. It will fall into futility, for life will lead nowhere but to corruption and death (Rom. 8:20–21).

A moment will come when the history of creation will reach the goal God assigned to it in the beginning. Until it does reach that goal, creation waits and suffers like a woman giving birth. This comparison had already been used in earlier speculations concerning the coming of the messianic kingdom. The image conveys the idea of great joy and immense newness coming to pass through intense but liberating suffering. The truth of the image is not susceptible of experimental proof. Only faith can discern in events the movement toward an end that transcends them. "We" are the ones who "know" this (Rom. 8:22). Therefore we can state, in speaking of the meaning of history, what the suffering creation is still ignorant of.

The knowledge available to us today about the origin of the earth and the human species, however incomplete it may be, does not allow us to establish a simple causal relation between man's revolt against God and the existence of the various ills which afflict nature. These ills existed, at least in certain forms, before the appearance of man; they are still observable today in spheres where it is impossible to connect them with human sin. What is more, they are in many cases the necessary condition and hence, as it would appear, the natural basis, for the very life of the creative process. Did Paul plainly attribute these ills in their totality to the fall of man, as has been generally supposed? This question must be asked, because the exegesis of the text does not necessarily require that this was his thought. . . .

We find ourselves in quite a different context of thought when we read Rom. 8:18–23. Here creation is envisaged as being "in travail." We may indeed suppose that this painful condition is the consequence of the fall of man; but this is not clearly contained in the texts themselves. For what creation longs to be delivered from is corruption (phthora). Now Paul considered that the plan of God for the world ordained that the physical should be first and the spiritual second (I Cor. 15:45); which is tantamount to saying, as the Apostle adds, that the perishable comes first and the imperishable later. These notes, unfortunately very brief, are in harmony with the texts of Genesis. Creation was intended to be mastered by man who is the image of God so that it might pass from the physical and perishable stage to the spiritual and imperishable one. Man himself, created mortal, was destined to share in divine life. His disobedience deprived him of that supreme good and at the same time it thwarted creation of the good which it would have received from a humanity responsive to its divine vocation. . . .

The intervention of sin into the world may nevertheless have had disastrous effects. Unfortunately it is impossible for us to assess these exactly, since we can have no idea of what humanity might have become if its development had taken place in accordance with the plan of God. It is equally impossible to know what would be our relations with nature and our "lesser brethren" on the same hypothesis. In any event, it is clear that in the line of development from the physical to the spiritual which creation was intended to traverse (I Cor. 15:45–46) man has not progressed as he should have done. . . .

In consequence, when he meditates on his position in the world, how can man escape the painful consciousness of his responsibility in the sight of God for the control of the creative process that was entrusted to him, beginning with the control of his own body? And in view of the new vistas which are opened up to the eye of faith by the insertion into the world of creation of those potentialities of new life disclosed in Jesus Christ, how should he resist Paul's conclusion that the creation is awaiting from the new man in Christ the means of at last realizing its own original vocation?[3]

EPISTLES TO THE COLOSSIANS AND EPHESIANS

An indispensable presupposition of Paul's preaching of the good news is, as we have been seeing, the idea that the salvation brought by Christ has an historical dimension. This conception finds quasiphilosophical formulation in the writings of his later years, the Epistles to the Colossians and Ephesians.

In Colossians 1:15–16 Paul speaks of Christ as "the first-born of all creatures. In him everything in heaven and on earth was created, things visible and invisible, whether thrones or dominations, principalities or powers; all were created through him and for him." It is to be noted that the reason why Paul writes this letter is the attitude of certain innovators who had appeared at Colossae and were denying that Christ and his disciples could bring humankind a total "salvation." The spectacle of Christ himself being executed by the Romans and of the Apostles being constantly persecuted and in danger of death was being exploited by the innovators as an argument that Christ possessed no real power to save.

Paul is attempting, therefore, to show that Christ brings a complete and integral salvation; to this end he wants to present him as the center and axis of creation. He has no intention of separating Christ from the material world and putting him off in some region of the spirit; on the contrary, he strongly asserts the decisive dynamic presence of Christ at the very heart of creation, this last being here, as elsewhere in the Bible, presented as still in process of formation.

Christ, then, is "the beginning" (Cor. 1:18), for he inaugurates that decisive stage of human history that has for its goal the eschatological resurrection. Christ is "the first-born of the dead" (ibid.); he had joined the numberless throng of the dead, but departed from among them in his resurrection in which he anticipated, and became a pledge of, the resurrection of all who "die in Christ." This idea of the universal significance of Christ's resurrection in this new order of things is especially dear to Paul (cf. 1 Thess. 4:14; 1 Cor. 15:21; 2 Cor. 4:14; 5:15). (The phrase "first-born of the dead" will also be used in Rev. 1:5.)

The whole was made by Him for [His] own sake. The Word which is attested for us in Holy Scripture, the story of Israel, of Jesus Christ and His Church, is the first thing, and the whole world with its light and shadow, its depths and its heights is the second. By the Word the world exists. A marvelous reversal of our whole thinking! Don't let yourselves be led astray by the difficulty of the time-concept, which might well result from this. The world came into being, it was created and sustained by the little child that was born in Bethlehem, by the Man who died on the Cross of Golgotha, and the third day rose again. *That* is the Word of creation, by which all things were brought into being.[4]

In Ephesians 1:10, Paul presents the history of salvation as a series of "moments" or "saving events" (*kairoi*) that take place in the course of time and reach their climax in the "recapitulation" (*anakephalaiosis*) or end point of history. The moment of recapitulation is evidently the Parousia of Christ and the eschatological resurrection. Saint Irenaeus, who has a deep understanding of Paul and whose own thought is so close to that of the Apostle, gives a very simple explanation of the recapitulation idea. In summing up the essentials of the creed which he claims the Church has received "from the hands of the Apostles and disciples," he lists as a basic article of faith "the Parousia of Christ in the heavens in the glory of the Father, in order to recapitulate all reality and to raise up every human being."[5]

In Colossians and Ephesians, Paul is trying to counter the minimizing tendencies of the innovators by showing the full dimensions of Christ and his good news. In so doing he situates the "mystery" in the context of the universal history of creation.

The term "mystery of God" (Col. 2:2) or "of Christ" (Eph. 3:4; Col. 4:3) or "of the Gospel" (Eph. 6:19) refers to the events of the last times; these events have already been determined in the divine plan but are kept hidden, except to the extent that God has deigned to reveal them beforehand to his servants, the prophets, until the moment when they come to pass. The "mystery", then, was not something unforeseen in the original plans of God; much less was it a chance product of history. On the contrary: "The mysterious design . . . for ages was hidden in God, the Creator of all" (Eph. 3:9).

The qualifying phrase, "the Creator of all," seems to be connected with the very existence of the mystery within the mind of God. By this I mean that when Paul applies to God the words "the Creator of all," he is stressing the fact that he in whom the mystery has been hidden since the beginning of time is identically the creator of the universe. He is telling us that there is a positive connection between the very creation of the world and the mystery or plan of God which, as he says elsewhere, was conceived "before the ages" (1 Cor. 2:7) or "before the world began" (Eph. 1:4).

The mystery, as Paul presents it, passes, as it were, through three stages. The first is its conception in the mind of the creator: "the mysterious design which for ages was hidden in God, the Creator of all" (Eph. 3:9). The second stage embraces the whole of the pre-Christian period: The mystery was "unknown to men in former ages but [is] now revealed by the Spirit to the holy apostles and prophets" (Eph. 3:5). The third and final stage is its historical fulfillment. The mystery is at work within the history of humankind and the universe; it permeates the very structure of the cosmos. As for Christians, "May charity be the root and foundation of your life. Thus you will be able to grasp fully, with all the holy ones, the breadth and length and height and depth of Christ's love, and experience this love which surpasses all knowledge, so that you may attain to the fullness of God himself" (Eph. 3:17–19).

In this last text Paul is referring to the splendor of the great building whose foundations have already been laid and in which

Christians have already taken up their abode. The building is as large as the universe, it has the dimensions of creation itself, and the idea that Christ "fills the universe in all its parts" runs throughout the two letters we are discussing (Eph. 1:23; 3:19; 4:10, 13; Col. 2:9–10). Christ is the "fullness" *(pleroma)* of God, not only because he himself is filled with the divine but because he fills everything else. And the Church is the "fullness" of Christ, not only because Christ fills it with all his blessings but also because through it and by means of it he fills all else, for it "is his body, the fullness of him who fills the universe in all its parts" (Eph. 1:23).

Love is a moving force that has its origin in the Father, passes by way of Christ, and abides in the Church whose inner form is the Holy Spirit. From thence it is to penetrate the whole cosmos and produce God's masterpiece, creation transformed into a gigantic cosmic cathedral. This temple is now being built by the pleromatic action of Christ through his Church; the immense building, a living thing whose vital principle is love, is gradually arising as Christ "fills the universe in all its parts." The Christian, therefore, may not narrow his theological vision to the narrow immediate context in which he lives, but must cultivate a panoramic vision that embraces creation in all its immensity.

The mystery of Christ is, in the last analysis, the mystery of the Gospel, that is, of the divine plan to bring human history to its maturity and biological fulfillment through the proclamation of the good news that, in and through Christ, people may overcome their "alienations," achieve their existential fulfillment, and enter into the new and final creation.

Thus, through prayer, through his sheer presence and then through his sharing in God's creative action, the Christian works to transform the world into a sacrament and human culture into an ikon of the heavenly Jerusalem into which "the treasures and wealth of the nations shall be brought" (Rev. 21:26). As history shows, this work is never finished and must always be begun anew, for its results will be fully manifested only at the Parousia. The most perfect fruit of that work is holiness, and holiness will always be a painful achievement as long as all do not possess it. To become holy is to discover that communion expresses the very structure of the person; to become holy means, therefore, that a person will pray that the holiness of him who alone is the Holy One may enlighten all people and, through them, the universe in its entirety. Of course, the saints do experience after death the "sabbath rest": "They shall find rest from their labors, for their good works accompany them" (Rev. 14:13). But even this rest is a waiting, and Christ himself, says Origen, experiences a kind of unfulfillment as he waits for the completion of his body, the Church: "for there is but a single body and it waits for . . . its perfect blessedness" (Homilies on Leviticus 7:2). Meanwhile the heavenly waiting of the saints becomes a collaboration with Christians on earth for the building of the kingdom. . . .

When the Christian gives his life, whether all at once or day by day, he should realize that through his defeats on earth he is rebuilding a world that will last through eternity. . . .

Christians know that earthly values are relative. That enables them to use them in a proper way and without risk of falling into idolatry. The person who knows that all things die, and that therefore all need salvation, can love as he should. Only his sacrifice in behalf of the realities he knows to be relative can give them an eternal value.[6]

NOTES

1. Leenhardt, Epistle to the Romans, pp. 218–19.

2. Pierre Duhem, Le système du monde (Paris: Hermann, 1914), 2:295–96.

3. Leenhardt, Epistle to the Romans, pp. 223–25.

4. Karl Barth, Dogmatics in Outline, trans. G.T. Thompson (London: SCM, 1949; New York: Harper Torchbook, 1959), pp. 57–58.

5. Irenaeus, Against Heresies, I, 10; PG 7:549.

6. Olivier Clément, Transfigurer le temps: Notes sur le temps à la lumière de la tradition orthodoxe (Neuchâtel: Delachaux et Niestle, 1959), pp. 206–07, 208, 212–13.

CHAPTER 8

LOVE OF NEIGHBOR: THE MORALITY OF "INCARNATION"

The call of God takes concrete form in a fact that is the source of salvation: the presence of Christ within history. This saving presence is brought to bear, not from outside, but through immersion in the defective reality that requires salvation. For this reason, the Church's way of salvation, summed up in the morality of love, must be one of "incarnation" that follows the model of Christ's own saving *kenosis* or self-emptying.

THE "SOCIOLOGICAL" INCARNATION

Christianity differs from other religions not exclusively or even chiefly in the content of its dogma and moral teaching, but in its reference to a historical fact that commands the very course of history. This fact is the great event of our complete salvation being brought to us by Christ.

The human person is a being who is thrust into life and inevitably subjected to a twofold alienation: moral and physical wretchedness, with the physical wretchedness ending in death. The "good news" is the proclamation of our complete liberation: Christ has come to make it possible for us to be entirely freed of our alienations.

The liberation might have been offered by Christ from outside, as it were, that is, by a Christ who was already living a fulfilled human life, one that was exempted from the human wretchedness he came to redeem. But events took a different course, for the "savior" chose to immerse himself fully in this wretched human condition. In the language of the Bible, "flesh," as we have seen, does not mean the material part of the person but the whole person as viewed in his pervasive wretchedness. This is why the New Testament writers are astounded, not that God became man, but that Christ—the Savior—became flesh, which is to say a wretched human being. The Gospel narratives show Jesus fully subject to the human condition in all its pitifulness, while John and Paul expressly assert his intention to commit himself to a "sociological incarnation": "The Word became flesh and made his dwelling among us" (John 1:14).

The basic structure of Pauline thought is determined by his teaching on the two Adams. Christ, the incarnate Son of God, might have saved the Adamic person from outside, that is, while remaining "rich" (2 Cor. 8:9) or retaining the "form of God" and his "glory" (Phil. 2:6, 11). He preferred however a way of salvation that involved his "enfleshment." In this way he became a second Adam. The first Adam had brought humankind to catastrophe from inside, that is, by acting within the bonds of solidarity with the human race as a whole. Jesus would act in the same circumstances, but to the opposite end; he would immerse himself in the contaminated waters of human history and would share in all human alienations, not simply as a romantic gesture of solidarity but in order to emerge from those waters and free himself of those alienations as a forerunner who would draw after him the rest of a new human race.

Nowhere in Paul (nor in the rest of the New Testament, for that matter) do we find the suffering and death of Christ presented as the cause of human salvation without reference to the resurrection. If Christ had been simply a noble companion in the imprisonment and suffering of the condemned Adamic person and had not finally broken the chains (of sin and death) for himself and his fellows, then there would (logically) have been no salvation. "If Christ was not raised, your faith is worthless. You are still in your sins, and those who have fallen asleep in Christ are the deadest of the dead. If our hopes in Christ are limited to this life only, we are the most pitiable of men" (1 Cor. 15:17–19).

On this basis Paul builds his theology of the *kenosis* or self-emptying by which Christ wrought our salvation. Christ is a savior from inside. His immersion in the contaminated waters of history and his intense struggle with the waves that finally overwhelmed him would have a happy ending only in his emergence into unending life in the resurrection. Christ will come forth victorious, and, since he is the rightful new Adam, he will carry with him to victory all those who are united to him: Christ "died for all so that those who live might live no longer for themselves, but for him who for their sakes died and was raised up" (2 Cor. 5:15). "None of us lives as his own master and none of us dies as his own master. While we live we are responsible to the Lord, and when we die we die as his servants. Both in life and in death we are the Lord's" (Rom. 14:7–9).

For this reason, after presenting Christ as the second Adam who brings all humankind with him on his journey from sin to justification and from death to life (Rom. 5), the Apostle goes on to explain baptism as an incorporation into the death of Christ (Rom. 6). The Christian continues the daily process of dying, as does any Adamic person, but there is nonetheless a great difference, for he dies the death of Christ, that is, a death from which he shall someday come forth to life (Rom. 6:4–5).

The saving self-emptying of Christ is described by Paul in a very vivid, we might even say scandalous, way. Thus: God made him "to be sin" (2 Cor. 5:21; Rom. 8:3); Christ "has delivered us from the power of the law's curse by himself becoming a curse for us" (Gal. 3:13); he has restored to us our divine inheritance by himself becoming one of the disinherited (cf. Gal. 4:4–5). In other words, the way in which Christ chose to liberate or save us was to take on our state of accursedness; in some sense, he became sin (2 Cor. 5:21; Rom. 8:3) and submitted to death with all its terrors (Phil. 2:8).

Paul illustrates the state of accursedness that Christ made his own, with a pertinent quotation from Deuteronomy (21:23): "Accursed is anyone who is hanged on a tree" (cf. Gal. 3:13). A person who dies by being "hanged on a tree" was doubly unclean: because he was dead (death was a source of legal uncleanness) and because he was a sinner (such a death was inflicted because a person was "guilty of a capital offense" [Deut. 21:22]). In other words, if to the death which every person had to die there was added the circumstance that the death was inflicted for a capital offense, then the curse of God was total. Consequently, Christ, being "hanged on a tree" as a malefactor, plumbed the very depths of the human condition that could be qualified as cursed by God, for he was now swallowed up both by sin and by death.

This self-emptying of Christ, who had become a "curse," was recompensed by the salvation that was its happy outcome. Christ has accepted the law's curse so that "the blessing bestowed on Abraham might descend on the Gentiles" (Gal. 3:14). The curse consisted of sin and death; the blessing, in justice and life. The self-emptying of Christ is effective for salvation insofar as it ends in victory: "If Christ was not raised, your faith is worthless. You are still in your sins" (1 Cor. 15:17).

If Christ's death has only been a romantic gesture of solidarity with his afflicted fellow human beings, it would not have brought justification and life. The redemptive value of Christ's death is due to the fact that death opens into a totally restored life.

In Galatians 4:1–3, Paul applies to humankind as saved by Christ the metaphor of the liberated son. Under Roman and Hellenistic law, as long as the son of the house was still a child he lived with the slaves and was subject to the will of a slave who acted as a nurse (paidagogos). When he reached the age of sixteen, the boy put on the "robes of a man" and was taken into his father's apartments; henceforth he was treated as a son and not as a slave. In the application of the comparison, humankind before Christ's coming is the son who is still a child; when Christ comes, this person passes from the control of slaves (the law and "the elements of the world") into the immediate presence of his Father. But Christ is the first to make this transition and he starts it by living with slaves.

Paul speaks, with reference to Christ, of "the designated time" (chronos Gal. 4:4; more literally, "the fullness of time"); in the logic of the comparison, this "designated time" should correspond to the time set (verse 2) for donning the robes of a man.

Throughout the New Testament there is a clear distinction between *chronos* and *kairos. Chronos* is time in the sense of the
chronological succession of events whose lineal sequence constitutes history. *Kairos,* on the other hand, is time in the sense of
opportune moment or "the time for" something; the *kairoi* (plural)
are those various significant moments in the history of salvation
that have been foreordained by God.[1]

Paul is simply saying that the time (*chronos*) had come within
the historical sequence of events for God the Father to carry out his
intention of "freeing" his son and restoring him to the life of
sonship. But by the very fact that God thus intervenes, this particular moment of *chronos,* this particular link in the continuous chain
of history, in which a simple Jew was born just like so many others
in the reign of Augustus, becomes a *kairos,* or a decisive moment.
It becomes the first and determinative *kairos* that will be followed
by a series of other *kairoi.* The fullness or completion of these (cf.
Eph. 1:10: literally, "the plan for the fulfillment of the significant
moments [*kairoi*]") is, evidently, the completion that is brought
about by the final coming of Christ.

The appearance of Christ within human history (within
chronos) was not merely a breakthrough from above, so that it
only peripherally and tangentially came in contact with the events
that made up world history. No, the "Son of God" emerged from
within history like any other person; he was a man burdened with
all the effects of human alienation, "born of a woman, born under
the law" (Gal. 4:4).

What Paul is emphasizing here is not the simple fact of birth, but
the constant, normal result of such a birth. The "Son of God" was
born of a woman; therefore he was like any other person, he was
completely a person and fully involved in the historical situation
that can be described as a state of accursedness. Such an insis-
tence on the Son of God being genuinely involved in human
history is essential to Pauline thought, for humankind as a whole is
in some sense identified with Christ (Gal. 3:28) and forms, along
with him, a single unified whole. The passage of this one human
race from a condition of slavery to a condition of sonship is to take
place "in Christ." For this reason, Christ must himself be fully a
part of human history, with nothing to weaken his oneness with

the rest of humankind. In the first part of his existence Christ shares the servile condition ("born of a woman") so that he may be able to transform human history from within.

The Pauline statement that God sent forth his Son acquires its full meaning in the light of his further words about the Son's redemptive mission: "so that we might receive our status as adopted sons" (Gal. 4:4–5). As the family was conceived in antiquity, adoption was a means provided by religion and law for childless couples to perpetuate the family line and thus to assure continuity in the worship of the family gods and the transmission of material wealth. For a couple to adopt, they either had to have no sons of their own or, if they had such, they had to expel them from the family and to surrender all parental power over them (this process was called *apokeryxis,* or disinheritance[2]).

Such is the juridical conception that clearly forms the basis for Paul's thinking in this part of Galatians, for he clearly seems to be thinking of a "disinheritance." In a mysterious way that is beyond our power to comprehend, God casts out his own Son (though admittedly the metaphor cannot be pushed to any metaphysical conclusion).

We must remember, however, that the main thing in Paul's mind is the unity of Christ with the human race that he saves. When Christ becomes part of the human tragedy and is in a sense disinherited by his Father (cf. Matt. 27:46; Mark 15:34), he must, as it were, win back, even for himself, what he had, in some ineffable way, lost; he must make his way out of the sin and death that he had made his own in order to bestow a new existence upon humankind.

LAWS OF "REDEMPTION THROUGH INCARNATION"

The "sociological enfleshment" of Christ, of which we have been speaking, was accepted as a way of liberation from the very wretchedness Christ had made his own. Paul expounds a law of redemption through incarnation, which has three stages:

1. The Savior has a redemptive power that the oppressed masses of humankind do not.

Christ "was in the form of God" (Phil. 2:6);

He "was rich" (2 Cor. 8:9);

He "did not know sin" (2 Cor. 5:21);

He was "God's Son" (Rom. 8:3; Gal. 4:4);

He was the "Christ" (Gal. 3:13).

2. The Savior enters fully into the human condition from which he must rescue humankind.

Christ "emptied himself and took the form of a slave, being born in the likeness of men''; he accepted suffering and death in its most shameful form (Phil. 2:7–8);

He "made himself poor" (2 Cor. 8:9);

"God made him. . . to be sin" (2 Cor. 5:21);

"God sent his Son in the likeness of sinful flesh" (Rom. 8:3);

"Born of a woman, born under the law" (Gal. 4:4);

"Becoming a curse for us" (Gal. 3:13).

3. The Savior did not accept this wretched human condition simply as a gesture of solidarity but in order to effect humankind's salvation from within by first "saving" himself and then others.

After his self-emptying, now "Jesus Christ is Lord" (Phil. 2:11);

We have "become rich by his poverty" (2 Cor. 8:9);

"God made him . . . to be sin, so that in him we might become the very holiness of God" (2 Cor. 5:21);

"God sent his Son in the likeness of sinful flesh as a sin offering, thereby condemning sin in the flesh, so that just demands of the law might be fulfilled in us" (Rom. 8:3–4);

"Born of a woman . . . so that we might receive our status as adopted sons" (Gal. 4:4–5);

"Born under the law, to deliver from the law those who were subjected to it" (Gal. 4:4–5);

"Becoming a curse for us . . . so that through Christ Jesus the blessing bestowed on Abraham might descend on the Gentiles in Christ Jesus" (Gal. 3:13–14).

This, then, is how Christ made possible our redemption, but he requires cooperation from us. To be a Christian means that a person takes an active part in carrying out the task of redeeming humankind in the course of history. Moreover, as we have seen, the redemption in question is a total one; the goal is the maximum elimination of moral and physical wretchedness. No partial fulfillment of the task is acceptable.

At present, however, the task is being carried on in a heretical way inasmuch as distorted forms of redemption are being pursued:

1. *Purely physical redemption:* It is of course true that no theory of human development fails to take into account, at least at the level of overall policy, some improvement and elevation of humankind. But when it comes to practice, decisions are often motivated by a pragmatism that is at times grossly materialistic. The outcome of such efforts at a purely physical kind of redemption is always the permanent, organized exploitation of the weaker individual or class to the profit of those who have force, money, or power at their disposal.

2. *Purely moral redemption:* This is the most harmful of "Christian" temptations; unfortunately, people not infrequently succumb to it. Gnostic anthropologies have influenced the very concepts of redemption and salvation and emptied them of a good deal of their content. Redemption comes to be understood simply as a rescue from sin; no further attention is paid to the rich content of the Christian message insofar as it proclaims the complete salvation of humankind within history and by means of human effort that has been sanctified through baptism.

3. *Paternalistic redemption:* By this I mean the effort, already analyzed, to carry on the redemptive process from outside, from the safe vantage-point of self-sufficiency, and without personally descending into the depths of that wretchedness from which humankind must be redeemed.

4. *"Romantic" redemption:* This is the naive and ineffective procedure in which a person enters indeed into the wretchedness of his fellows, but has failed to acquire the resources that will enable him to emerge from that state.

The resources in question are:

Spiritual: a deeply religious attitude and prayerfulness. One who would share in the activity of redeeming must first have the indispensable resources of an intense spiritual life. Holiness, at least as a goal that is seriously pursued, is an antecedent condition for which nothing else can make up.

Intellectual: the greater the wretchedness to be shared, the greater the intellectual preparation needed. The goal is real improvement along the lines of an integral human development, and this requires shrewd and discriminating reflection in all areas.

Social: the ability to effect, from within, the advancement of the oppressed, sinful, or suffering group of people of which the "redeemer" has become a part.

The possession of such resources guarantees the success of the essentially Christian effort at "redemption through incarnation." Merely romantic gestures of incarnation have too often led to demagogy and cast discredit on the authentic methods to be found in the Gospels and Paul.

THE MARXIST SECULARIZATION OF "REDEMPTION THROUGH INCARNATION"

Camus rightly observes that, in Nietzsche's view, "socialism is only a degenerate form of Christianity."[3]

More recently Nicolas Berdyaev defended the same thesis with a great wealth of detail. In his opinion, the neglect by Christians of such essentially evangelical attitudes as "redemption through incarnation" made it possible for Marxism to take them over while completely secularizing them.

Christians ought to be permeated with a sense of the religious importance of the elementary daily needs of men, the vast masses of men, and not to despise those needs *from the point of view of an exalted spirituality.* Communism is a great mentor for Christians; it is a frequent reminder to them of Christ and the Gospels and of the prophetic elements in Christianity.[4]

The great Marxist theoreticians themselves acknowledge the value of historical Christianity, to the extent that Christianity was the work of the masses. Engels claimed that "Christianity, like every great revolutionary movement, was made by the masses."[5]

The collapse of the ancient world undoubtedly caused a stagnation, that is, cultural regression in the areas of development and discovery. Christianity, on the other hand, notably broadened the bases of culture in the masses and spread abroad among the lowest levels of the populace ideas that had been developed in the ancient world but hitherto were reserved for a cultural elite. For example, the idea of the unity of the human race had been maintained by the Stoics and Epicureans, but only Christianity would make it the possession of all, Romans and barbarians alike.[6]

Yet Marxists refuse to acknowledge the Christian origins of many of their basic ideas. Lenin admits, in ironic tones, that certain "good Fathers," concerned as they are for "our salvation," do not hesitate to regard Christianity as one of the sources of Marxism. What a pious contradiction! Marxism is indeed (Lenin goes on) the outcome of the whole culture of the past, and this culture undoubtedly developed through a long period of time in religious forms. But for centuries now religious culture has had to yield ground to a new secular, rational, and scientific culture that is essentially antireligious. It is out of this new culture, not theology, that Marxism has emerged.[7]

Nonetheless it is evident that Christian patterns of thought live on in Marxism, especially in the messianic and redemptive interpretation of the function of the proletariat. Henri Lefèbvre writes:

In modern class society one class is assigned a privileged role in the achievement of the goal. That class is the proletariat. It alone can by its action bring an end to human alienation, and *the reason is that it lives and suffers that alienation to the full.* It alone can free society and the person by freeing itself, for it alone bears the full weight of oppression and exploitation. . . . Marxist humanism is neither sentimental nor weepy. Marx was not inclined toward the proletariat because it was oppressed and because he felt sorry for that oppression. Instead, he showed how and why the proletariat could free itself from oppression and thus open the way to the fulfillment of all human potentialities. Marxism is not interested in the proletariat insofar as the proletariat is weak (that is the motivation of "charitable" people, of some utopians, of "paternalistic" people, whether sincere or insincere), but insofar as it is strong; not insofar as it is ignorant but insofar as it can assimilate knowledge and enrich it in turn; not insofar as it has been forced into inhuman conditions by the bourgeoisie but insofar as it bears within itself the future of humankind and rejects that bourgeoisie as itself inhuman. In short, Marxism sees in the proletariat the guarantee of its own future and its own possibilities.[8]

We cannot deny that Marxism has levelled fully justified criticisms at the paternalism that refuses incarnation yet claims to be able to redeem humankind. Nor can we deny that Marxism is getting at the very root of the problem when it stresses the necessity of seeking the salvation of the masses from within by making the masses not only the recipient of salvation but the means to it as well. In brief, Marxism has attempted to reassert the value of redemption through incarnation. But has it itself succeeded?

Albert Camus makes some basic points in this regard:

The idea of a mission of the proletariat has not, so far, been able to formulate itself in history: this sums up the failing of the Marxist prophecy. . . . His [Marx's] error lay only in believing that extreme poverty, and particularly industrial poverty, could lead to political maturity. . . .

The proletariat has had no other historical mission but to be betrayed. The workers have fought and died to give power to the military or to intellectuals who dreamed of becoming military and who would enslave them in their turn. . . .

Autocracy is its [revolutionary action's] enemy, whose main source of strength is the police force, which is nothing but a corps of professional political soldiers. The conclusion is simple: "The struggle against the political police demands special qualities, demands professional revolutionaries." The revolution will have its professional army as well as the masses, which can be conscripted when needed. This corps of agitators must be organized before the mass is organized. A network of agents is the expression that Lenin uses, thus announcing the reign of the secret society and of the realist monks of the revolution: "We are the Young Turks of the revolution," he said, "with something of the Jesuit added." From that moment the proletariat no longer has a mission. It is only one powerful means, among others, in the hands of the revolutionary ascetics.[9]

This amounts to saying that Marxism has quickly succumbed to the same defect for which it so sharply criticizes Christianity: The "saviors" of the proletarian masses have taken their position outside these masses and refused to accept the implications of the ''redemption through incarnation'' which they so highly praise. On the other hand, within the contemporary Church there is a restless longing for ''redemptive incarnation,'' and the Marxists recognize the fact. But the Marxists claim that this ''neo-Christian'' stirring is not the result of the essential principles of Christ's message, but of an attempt to imitate the Marxist way.

The God of the theologians and the modern poets would be less concerned with the poor and with the hopes and action of the militants, had not the poor (and especially the *atheistic* poor) first become concerned with themselves and had they not turned their hopes into practical reality. Conversely, the reason why contemporary Christians like to represent Christ in the guise of a worker is that *they may share* the hopes of the poor and the warmth of their militancy. The humanistic reinterpretation of religious themes makes it easier for these believers to take part in modern social action and even, in some cases, to take part in revolutionary action. . . . Contemplative attitudes are thus giving way, among believers, to militant attitudes, which increasingly lead to explicit involvement. The commandment of love is being given political content, and charity a social dimension that had hitherto been overlooked. The religious pharisaism of the ruling classes in Christian society is being ruthlessly attacked by believers themselves; we need only think of Roualt (especially his *Miserere*), Bernanos, Bergman, Fellini, Mauriac, and Kazantzakis. The *behavior* of the progressive Christian *seems* at least to be like that of the Communist.[10]

But the impartial study we have made of ''redemption through incarnation'' in Paul makes it clear that the Marxist claim concerning the origin of the ''new'' attitude of many Christians is not justified. It is undoubtedly true that Marxism can serve to wake us from our slumber. But we need only get to the heart of the Christian message in order to see that the present militancy of Christians springs logically from the New Testament teaching on redemption.

BLESSED ARE THE POOR

The whole Bible from Amos to St. James and from Deuteronomy to Jesus considers poverty (and the word has an extension greater than the simple privation of money) as an extreme state disturbing to our conscience. The correctives proposed in the inspired pages are dated. No claim is made that their repetition and slavish imitation will suffice until the end of time. However, in their recommendations, there is more than realism. In spite of a certain tendency (fairly localized, in our opinion) to equate the poor man and the sinner, there is the observation that the poor become religious more easily than the rich, because they are less likely to be self-sufficient and consequently closer to God. This is notably true of those ''little ones'' so dear to biblical authors, the poor who are some-where in between opulence and indigence. This is a theme of Proudhon clearly enunciated in the Old Testament. In any case, the critique of riches, made from a religious point of view, never ceased from the prophets to Jesus. It is He who, having chosen poverty as a means of the redemption, consecrated it as a value. Henceforth, each poor man, with his own special kind of poverty, is a reminder and, as it were, a sacrament of the great Poor Man proclaimed by the Second-Isaiah.[11]

That the ''poor'' are the intended hearers of the good news will be readily understood if we bear in mind the comprehensive conception of salvation that is sustained throughout the Bible. For the poor are the alienated, the dispossessed, who recognize their own radical inability to get out of their sorry state and therefore hope for a God who will save them.

The Beatitudes are an expression of the messianic hope of the Old Testament. When John the Baptist asked Jesus whether he was ''He who is to come'' (Matt. 11:3), Jesus had only to refer to texts of Isaiah which expressed the age-old hope of all the dispossessed (Isa. 26:19; 29:18–19; 35:5–6).

In this line of thought, the poor person is ''blessed,'' because as a result of the proclamation of the good news he will cease to be poor. The kingdom of God is meant precisely for him, since he needs that kingdom and *knows* that he needs it. For the kingdom of God, as we have seen, does not mean a purely moral liberation but the saving of the person from all his alienations and especially from the permanent alienation of death.

At the same time, however, throughout both the Old and the New Testaments a curse is pronounced upon riches. For, more than anything else, they are regarded as an obstacle to the progress of God's kingdom within human history. ''It is easier for a camel to pass through a needle's eye than for a rich man to enter the kingdom of God'' (Matt. 19:24). ''Worldly anxiety and the lure of money choke it [the word of God] off. Such a one produces no yield" (Matt. 13:22). "You cannot give yourself to God and money" (Luke 16:13). "None of you can be my disciple if he does not renounce all his possessions" (Luke 14:33). "Up to this very hour we [apostles] go hungry and thirsty, poorly clad, roughly treated, wandering about homeless. We work hard at manual labor" (1 Cor. 4:11–12; cf. 2 Cor. 11:9–27; Phil. 4:11–14).

How can the gospel be a proclamation of liberation for the poor and at the same time a pressing call to choose poverty?

The apparent contradiction vanishes when we look at it from the viewpoint of evangelical morality, which makes love of neighbor the hinge on which all turns.

The gospel is first and foremost the proclamation and implantation of love. Love is not a simple movement of affection; it contains the serious intention of freeing the neighbor from all that oppresses him. One of the things, however, that is most responsible for oppression is the lack of the material things one needs in order to develop himself as a person. Such poverty depersonalizes and is inherently immoral. For this reason Christians must put up a bold fight to free their neighbor from such inhuman want. For this reason, too, the gospel declares the poor blessed, since it proclaims that they will be rescued from their poverty by God's kingdom.

As we have seen, the only effective way to redeem people is the way of sociological incarnation, that is, by immersion in the wretchedness from which we are to be liberated. Riches, as history makes clear, are very likely to foster egotism, for they build a wall around their possessor and make him insensitive to the wretchedness of his neighbor. Paternalistic gifts thrown in the dirty faces of the "poor out there" from the remote security of one's own abundance are a pharisaic pretense, a sacrilegious effort to substitute for authentic love of neighbor.

When Marxists attack us on the gound that our sermons act as a restraint upon progress by calling the poor blessed instead of urging them to escape from their wretched condition, the Marxists are attacking a caricature of Christianity. Unfortunately, the caricature has become widespread within Christianity itself in the course of recent centuries.

The Christian paradox consists in declaring blessed both *the poor person to be redeemed,* because he will at last leave his poverty behind, and *the poor person who redeems,* because the poverty he accepts will lessen the poverty of his neighbor.

If the beatitudes are understood without this reference to incarnation through redemption, they become nothing but poetic sarcasms heaped upon humankind as it bows beneath the weight of its immense alienations.

People of our day, especially the young, suffer from an affliction of spirit which we have elsewhere called "built-in anxiety." They are aware that they are responsible for the course of history; they look anxiously for some work that will be genuinely effective in hastening the progress of human life to the heights of fulfillment. When we Christians in brotherly affection take the hand of these contemporaries, we must not betray the dynamism of the gospel which is regulated by these laws of redemption through incarnation. We must resist the modern temptation to which the great social bodies are subject, that of forcibly imposing a new state of affairs and looking for visible success that will catch attention through numbers and mass demonstrations.

Our faith means a belief that the dynamism of the gospel, at work in small ways, will cause in the atoms which make up human history an explosion of life, joy, and love; and that these will permeate a world now ice-bound by egotism and victimized by pseudogreatness and pseudopower.

NOTES

1. Cf. Oscar Cullmann, *Christ and Time: The Primitive Christian Conception of Time and History,* trans. Floyd V. Filson, rev. ed. (Philadelphia: Westminster, 1964), pp. 38–40; G. Delling, "kairos," *Theological Dictionary of the New Testament,* 3:455–64.

2. Cf. F. Baudry, *Dictionnaire des antiquités grecques et romaines,* 1:75–79.

3. Camus, *The Rebel,* p. 69.

4. Nicolas Berdyaev, *The Origin of Russian Communism,* trans. R.M. French (London: Geoffrey Bles, 1937), p. 185; emphasis added.

5. Friedrich Engels, "The Book of Revelation," in Karl Marx and Friedrich Engels, *On Religion* (New York: Schocken, 1964), p. 207.

6. Verret, *Marxistes et religion,* p. 75.

7. Cf. V.I. Lenin, "The Three Sources and Three Component Parts of Marxism," in *Selected Works,* 3 vols. (New York: International Publishers, 1967), 1:41–45.

8. Lefèbvre, *Le Marxisme,* pp. 47, 49.

9. Camus, *The Rebel,* pp. 215, 218, 228.

10. Verret, *Marxistes et religion,* p. 186.

11. Albert Gelin, *The Poor of Yahweh,* trans. Kathryn Sullivan, R.S.C.J. (Collegeville: Liturgical Press, 1964), pp. 111–12.

EPILOGUE

Samuel Beckett has brutally challenged our vision of the person with a drama in which nothing happens. There is no plot and no denouement. Life is seen in all its raw reality, a meaningless tapestry which we see only close up and, as it were, inside out. People do not understand each other; worst of all, they bore each other.

The aim of Beckett is to open the way to a philosophy of boredom. People invent wars and let themselves be carried away by hatred, anger, and lust, simply in order to escape tedium and boredom. But in the depths of the human heart there is still left a weak expectation of a mysterious person—Godot—who is constantly putting off his coming and who finally does not come.

In this drama not only does nothing happen; at the end the curtain seems to fall for good and dash the last tiny hope. Yet, for all that, *Waiting for Godot* is not simply a negative, destructive work. It contains a message that is of immense importance for our generation.

The men who attempt to pull the strings of the human puppets have committed the unforgivable sin of acting like ostriches; they have hidden their heads in the sand and paid no attention to the reality that does not please them. They have imagined a human situation stripped of its real tragic elements and transformed into a fanciful object of knowledge. They have severely chastised the messengers reality has sent to them, although these messengers were simply recordings, reporting the hard facts of the tragic situation. They have preferred to listen to those who, like the servants of the aristocracy in another day, tell them what they want to hear: "Nothing new, my Lord!"

We Christians cannot allow ourselves the unforgivable sacrilege of evasion. We cannot flee the real, incomprehensible, absurd, paradoxical world and take refuge in our hieratic ghetto where we devote ourself to refined intellectual fencing and ready-made asceticism. Instead, we must immerse ourselves in the mire of existence, in that web of life where we can play our concrete, individual roles. For, only from that vantage point within the human tragic situation can we shout forth the gospel message of salvation and raise our voices in a splendid cry of hope.

Our lives and our efforts are all commanded and conditioned by an intense waiting for Godot. We wait for Christ, the first person of the new world, to come someday to crown our efforts and do away with the absurdity of our lives.

Our expectation is not simple nostalgia, but rather has a great efficacy. Our energies, consecrated now by the waters of baptism, can enable human effort to bring about an historical development that will allow Christ to come again. Christ will come when we make him come, when we have carried out our worldly task of constant improvement.

Our expectation does not reach its fulfillment through foolish polemics or by living a boring, meaningless life, but through ceaseless constructive toil that hastens the birth of that eternity with which our corruptible world is now pregnant.

Only thus will our waiting for Godot, that waiting which we cannot eliminate from our hearts, cease to be an absurdity.